The Secret Commission

A Novel

By

Michael A. Campbell

The Secret Commission
by Michael A. Campbell

Printed in the United States of America

ISBN 1-591609-98-4

Unless otherwise indicated, Bible quotations are taken from *The Holy Bible*, Authorized King James Version. World Bible Publishers, Inc. © 1989.

Xulon Press
www.XulonPress.com

Xulon Press books are available in bookstores everywhere, and on the Web at www.XulonPress.com.

To Bob –

I believe in miracles

– You're one of them

_um_ _h._ _Gill_

6-21-05

1

People are like roses, Angus McKendrick thought as he reached down to tend to one of his flowers. They were beautiful, fragile, and needed loving attention to reach their full blooming glory. As a minister, he knew that it was a lot of hard, thankless work, but the ultimate results were worth it.

Angus thought about the young girl he had helped last night. Jenny Thatcher had been living on the streets for over a year, moving from one homeless shelter to another. Tired and hungry, Jenny had pounded on the door of the rectory house around suppertime last night. Angus invited her to dinner, listened to her story, and then sent Jenny on her way with money for a train ticket for Albany. For Angus, it was all in a day's work, but he'd hoped somehow that the young lady would take what he said to her to heart.

It was a bright summer morning in New York. The summer had been good this year, and Angus' garden looked especially glorious. Angus was eighty years old now, and had absolutely no business puttering around in a garden at six in the morning, much less pastoring a church. Since there seemed to be no one willing to do either of these tasks, Angus McKendrick had stepped up to do the job. It never occurred to him that he was very good at being a pastor, or that his congregation loved him; he was simply too busy to worry about that, or about being too old.

Angus straightened up and stretched. His back wasn't too bad today, which was a blessing. All of the branches on the roses had been clipped and the dead stems cast aside, ready for disposal. His watch beeped, so he knew it was time to go into the church to get ready for the Morning Prayer. Angus loved the church in the morning, with the sun streaming through the stained glass rose window sending jeweled lights onto the plain oak cross over the altar.

He set the tools to the side of the wheelbarrow and started over to the front door of the church. It was then that Angus noticed a pool of something dark seeping from the bottom of the front door. The pool was rapidly spreading, spilling over the edges of the first step and onto the second. Angus was alarmed at the sight: the church was well over a hundred years old, but the plumbing and roof were sound. Everything had been fine when he had locked the church up at nine last night. Angus had no idea where this stain could be coming from.

He reached the steps, and climbed them, stepping carefully over the dark red stain. It was blood, and Angus could feel his heart start to pound slowly as he turned the key, opened the door, and stepped inside.

A gust of cold fetid air rushed out at Angus as he stepped across the threshold. He had never felt anything like that in his church before. As his eyes adjusted to the dim light, Angus could see the pool of blood extending from the front of the sanctuary all the way up to the altar. The hideous cold in his church cut through him, and his breath came in slow deep gasps.

The light over the sanctuary was out. This was the red light over the altar, which signified the eternal presence of God in his house. It was out, and on the cross was stretched out something. As Angus approached the altar, he saw what it was.

It was a crucified human being. The blood was streaming from the body, which was nailed to the cross at its wrists and feet. Angus saw the tortured body rise up and take a breath: the person was still alive. Reaching the steps of the altar, he stared up into the tortured face.

It was the face of Jenny Thatcher, the girl from last night.

Angus gasped and turned to run from the sanctuary to get to a phone to summon help. Then he noticed that there was someone else in the church. Something black and terrible detached itself from the pools of blackness next to the altar and moved towards him. Angus' heart exploded in pain as it came towards him, taking the form of someone who could not be here, but was...

Then his world went black.

It had been a bad night in the Compton Emergency Room, Gwen Jones thought as she sat down in her chair for the first time in twelve hours. She was about to take sip of very old rancid coffee, when the emergency radio erupted.

"Compton ER, Compton ER, this is Medic 19, over."

Gwen reached for the microphone. "Medic 19, this is Compton ER. Go ahead, over."

"Roger, Compton ER," the medic replied, a note of urgency in her voice. "We are coming to you emergency traffic with a twenty-two year old female in cardiac arrest. Patient was found nailed to a cross at Trinity Church. I say again, nailed to a cross. It took fire and EMS twenty minutes to remove the patient from the scene. Patient was semi-conscious and breathing when removed but has now gone into asystole. We are doing CPR and have established two large-bore IVs with normal saline. One amp epinephrine has been given along with atropine. The patient is intubated with good placement confirmed. Be advised, Compton, this patient has had the skin removed from the neck on down. Our ETA to your facility is less than two minutes. Do you copy? Over."

Gwen frowned. "Medic 19, did you say that the patient has no skin from the neck down?" She motioned for the ER doctor, Maggie White, to come over and listen to the call.

"Roger, Compton. She has no skin from the neck down," the medic replied. Maggie reached over and keyed the mike. "Medic 19, this is Med Control. Wrap the patient in burn sheets, and give me a ballpark height and weight."

"Roger, Compton. Height five-six, weight approximately fifty-five kilos." Maggie started rapidly doing some calculations in her head. "We need to call in the trauma team," she told Gwen. Get me four bags of normal saline spiked and on poles. I want the lab to have four units of O-negative blood ready for transfusion. I need Respiratory Therapy down here stat with a ventilator."

Gwen was about ready to issue orders to the staff (the other nurse working with her that night) when the radio broke in again with another call. "Compton ER, Compton ER, this is Medic 46. Do you read, over?"

Gwen groaned. "Medic 46, this is Compton ER. Go ahead, over."

"Roger, Compton. We are coming to your location emergency traffic with an eighty-year old patient taken from Trinity Church complaining of acute crushing chest pain. Patient is semi-conscious at this time. We have a large bore IV established in the left antecubital vein. We have administered three sprays of nitroglycerin with some relief noted. His monitor shows acute S-T changes in lead two. The patient is on 100% oxygen per facemask. Oxygen saturation is 95 %.We are three minutes ETA from your location. Do you have any further orders, over?"

"Roger, Medic 46," replied Maggie. "Give 4 milligrams of morphine IV. Bed 6 on arrival. Compton ER, out."

Roger, Compton. Medic 46 out."

At that moment, hell exploded into the Compton ER. The medics poured out of the ambulance, bringing Jenny Thatcher's body into the trauma bay. The burn sheets wrapping her body were already soaking wet with her body fluids. They lifted her off the stretcher and slid her onto the narrow ER bed. The cardiac monitor showed the deep spikes and valleys of the medic's chest compressions, but nothing else.

"We just pushed another amp of epinephrine before we pulled in." one of the medics told Dr. White. "So far nothing's worked."

"Okay, stop compressions for a moment and see where we're at," Maggie said calmly. The room fell silent for a moment. The monitor settled down into a flat line pattern. "How much fluid has she had?"

"Two liters so far." the paramedic responded.

"Okay, let's resume CPR. Hang another bag of normal saline. Where's my blood?" She asked Gwen, who ran out to the desk to call the lab. Maggie started to do a primary survey of the body in a quick, professional matter, all the while keeping tabs on the efforts of the medics as they worked.

She stopped at the abdomen. Lifting up the sheets, Maggie looked at Jenny Thatcher's body. "Stop CPR!" she commanded. The medics stopped and waited. Maggie slowly pulled the sheets back for a closer look.

"I'm calling the code. Does anyone have the time?" She said wearily, replacing the sheets.

"Seven-twenty, Doc." one of the medics said. "What's the deal?" Maggie White had the reputation of never quitting on resuscitation as long as there was a shred of hope.

"Come see for yourself, guys," Maggie said. "You can't live without any organs."

She pulled back the cover to reveal Jenny's abdomen. Her belly had been neatly sliced open, and most of her internal organs had been removed.

Medic 46 pulled up at this moment, and Angus McKendrick was wheeled into the treatment area. Gwen pulled the curtain around the trauma bay and started towards her next patient.

Jenny's body was left alone in the treatment room. There was nothing more they could do for her. The ER personnel needed to tend to the living. The Medical Examiner would tend to Jenny now.

Angus was barely aware of anything as he was wheeled into the treatment bay. He knew that he would never forget the horror of what he had seen in the church. Through the fog of pain clouding his mind, Angus could hear people talking and shouting as things were done to his body.

But it was the voice of the one he'd heard in the church kept reverberating in his mind over and over again. The only thing Angus could see with clarity was Jenny's crucified body as she struggled to catch one last dying breath...

Sid Drucker, The *Post's* crime editor, usually came in promptly at eight. He did this to beat the traffic, and also to get a firsthand account of the overnight events on the crime scene. Today was a complete snore: two homicides in the City, probably gang related, a scattered mix of fights and stabbings, nothing worth any kind of story. There was a weird story from out on Long Island: a homicide in a church in a place called Compton.

"Sid, there's a box that some guy left for you downstairs early this morning. I brought it up and put it by your desk." one of the night editors said as Sid came to his desk.

Sid yawned and decided to start by opening the box addressed from Compton. "What a coincidence: there was a story about

Compton today and this thing arrives for me." Tearing open the outer box, he saw that there was a sealed inner plastic container. "I wonder what it is?"

"Aren't you afraid of anthrax or bombs, Boss?" quipped one of the writers. "I'd be, after the way you trashed the Mayor's aunt the other day when she got picked up on a Drunk and Disorderly."

"Nah," Sid replied, opening the plastic container. A fetid odor of decay suddenly filled the room. He gasped and turned green as he backed away from the container, spilling its contents onto the floor. A single sheet of paper with writing on it fluttered out of the box. Drucker scooped up the letter before it could be soiled by the rapidly spreading puddle of body fluids and blood.

On the sheet was scrawled in a scraggly, rambling hand:

Dear Boss:
I hope you like my little anniversary gift to you and all the fine people at the scandal sheet you work for. Just wanted to drop you a note to let you know I've set up shop here in America for a while. I'll be cutting up whores and slags on a regular basis now until the Peelers pinch me. Last night was so much fun. I will post you on a regular basis on what I'm up to.
Tell Charlie Warren I'm waiting.

Yours,
Jack the Ripper

"Get that mess outta here!" he screamed, gagging and retching as the rest of the staff headed out the door. "Call the cops, someone!"

Jenny Thatcher's missing organs had been found.

David Stone had been awake since three in the morning. This had been his sleep pattern for the last three months. Ever since Karen died, he dreaded the small hours of the morning between three and six. That was when the dream happened, and the only way David could avoid it was to waken at three in the morning.

The dream always started out the same way. He was running along a dark, endless corridor next to his wife Karen, who was on a stretcher. She would be calling to him, "Help me, David, help me. It hurts so bad! Make it stop, David!"

David tried to hold onto her hand, tried to comfort her. "This can't be happening," he kept thinking as they rolled her stretcher into the ER treatment area. "It's okay, Karen, you'll be fine. It's just a little gas, or something." David said those words, but knew in his heart that something terrible was happening to his wife. They had only been married for three months when Karen found out she was pregnant. Now their happiness had been destroyed in one terrifying night of sudden pain.

David could feel her life slipping away from him. Karen's hands became ice cold, and her eyes glazed over. He was shoved away from her by the nurses and doctors crowding into the area with resuscitation equipment. Someone pulled him away into a small room. A short time later the doctor came in with the chaplain. David remembered staring up at the clock as they walked through the door. It was three in the morning when they came to tell him that Karen had died.

He would see her being carried away from him forever, down a long endless tunnel, and then he would wake up in tears, holding the covers and the pillow of a half-empty bed.

David stared out the window, watching the sky slowly brighten. The hours crept away from him, and he turned over to read the numbers on the clock. It was now six, and it was time to get ready for work. David knew it was the start of another long, endless day. He dragged himself over to the bathroom, showered, shaved, and dressed himself. Things now happened to him more out of reflex than anything else. He stared at the gaunt face looking at him in the mirror. David had lost so much weight that his gray eyes seemed to be in deep pools of shadow. His dark brown hair was now shot through with strands of gray.

Mechanically pouring himself a cup of coffee, David ate half of a muffin before going out to his car. The drive to work took ten minutes, during which he thought of nothing except how many minutes remained before he would drive back to the empty house.

"Dave, Carl wants to see you in his office." the desk sergeant said as David came through the station front door. David winced.

He knew what was coming. Since Karen's death three months ago, his work had slipped badly. The DA had probably filed another complaint on him, he thought bitterly as he knocked on Carl's door.

Carl Davis was the Chief of Police. He was David's best friend, and he was also David's boss. These two facts were currently warring inside of Carl as he looked at David. Karen's death had nearly destroyed his friend, and Carl was desperately worried.

David walked into Carl's office, knowing that this would be it. His eyes strayed to the back wall that was filled with certificates, awards, and pictures: Carl in the Army, Carl graduating from the FBI Academy, and so on. David was in some of these pictures. The good times they had had together came up from his past to accusingly mock him. David felt as though he'd let everyone down, and now it was time for him to face the consequences.

Carl tracked his friend's eyes as he glanced over the pictures. He had to do something for David, or he would lose him. Carl had lost friends this way before. Sometimes a death or divorce would just destroy a man or woman in a way that left them beyond repair. Carl finally decided: today is the day that David is either saved or he would leave the force.

"Dave, close the door," Carl said. David closed the door quietly. The sound of the busy police station softened, and the air became quiet and heavy. Carl settled back into his chair, searching for a way to begin.

"I got a call from the DA's office yesterday," he started, picking up a file folder. "The Morgan case you worked on: Sheila told me there was no way she could go to trial with the case you've put together. There are so many procedural mistakes and omissions that a judge would dismiss the case in five minutes. Sheila says that the whole thing needs to be done over from the ground up, and quickly. It's the worst work she's ever seen since she's been a District Attorney. I've looked it over, and I agree."

David reached for the file, but Carl moved it out of his reach. "I'm giving it to Joan Richards to finish. She's agreed, and the whole department is going to take on the rest of your case load, starting today."

David lurched to his feet. "Okay, Carl," he said hoarsely, "I'll have my resignation on your desk in half an hour." He fumbled in his pocket for his wallet, looking for his badge. Carl put up a restraining hand.

"Hold on," he growled, "what do you think you're doing? I don't want your badge, or your resignation. Sit down before you fall down. That's an order."

Carl paused for a moment before he continued: "David, we went through Basic, Special Forces training, and Desert Storm together. You saved my life half a dozen times. "People in this department respect you, and they respect your work." Carl's voice softened. "When Karen died, you took off exactly five days after her funeral. You were back at work the following Monday. No one, not even you, can change gears that fast. You gave yourself no time to grieve, no time to recover."

Carl reached into his desk and pulled out an envelope. "This is an airline ticket to the Virgin Islands. You are now officially on administrative leave, with pay. You are to go to your house, pack your bags and head for the airport. I have given orders to my department that if you don't comply with these instructions, you'll be carried to the plane in a patrol car in cuffs."

David just stared at him, not knowing what to say. Carl read his mind. "Everyone in the department pitched in on the tickets and hotel, Dave. Please take some time to heal. When you come back, we'll start over and get you back on your feet."

The telephone rang. Carl picked up the phone and snarled into the receiver: "I told you not to interrupt me! What? Okay, I'll get someone over there. Secure the crime scene and call the hospital. Make sure that body is not tampered with."

He hung up the phone and looked at David with a glint in his eye. "Looks like that trip is going to have to wait. We just got a murder case, and you're going to be the one to take it on. A girl was killed at Trinity Church at around six this morning. The minister found her barely alive and he wound up having a heart attack. She died at the ER at around seven-thirty. Head on over to the crime scene. Are you up to it?"

David smiled for the first time that day, "Yes sir, I'm ready. Thanks for caring."

"Get out of here before I have you arrested for loitering," growled Carl. "Just make sure that I'm not making a mistake in handing you this one."

David didn't bother to reply. He was already out the door.

He got into his car and drove down to Trinity. The church was located on a quiet side street just off of Main Street. Trinity always reminded David of those pictures of English country churches that his mother was so fond of. The last time he had been at the church was for Karen's funeral. The sight of the church started the memories welling back up into his mind.

The outside of the church was cordoned off with crime scene barrier tape, flanked by half a dozen patrol cars. The crime scene unit was already busy inside the church collecting evidence. The fire department had to be called in to remove Jenny Thatcher from the cross that she had been nailed to. The inside of the church was in chaos and reflected the desperation of their efforts.

Joan Richards, one of the detectives who doubled as the department's crime scene investigator, was obviously frustrated. "I'm not going to have much for you right now, Dave," she said as he came up to her inside the church. "Fire and EMS trampled over things pretty good in here. Of course at that time the girl was alive, and they were trying to save her." She handed him a wallet covered by a plastic bag. "I did find this on one of the front pews. It's the victim's wallet. It's got her name and home address."

"A thoughtful killer, how nice," said David, looking at the picture. "Jenny Thatcher: is she a local girl?"

"No," Joan replied, "Her ID lists her home address as Albany. The minister is Angus McKendrick. He's been here as long as I can remember. He's originally from England and came over here after the war."

"I know Father McKendrick. He did my wife's funeral a few months ago," David noted. Quickly changing the subject, he asked Joan about signs of forced entry.

"The door in the back has not been forced open," Joan replied, grateful that the subject had quickly veered off of personal issues.

"The front door is intact as well. There are no fingerprints on either entrance, other than the minister's prints and the ones left by EMS. I'm trying to figure out how someone could hoist a body up into the air and nail it to a cross without using any sort of ladder." She handed him another bag with four long, curiously shaped nails. "Ever see nails like these?"

"No," David said, studying the nails. "They look almost like they were hand made, don't they?"

"I've never seen anything like them before," said Joan. "These nails were used to nail that girl to the cross. They are definitely not commercial. Whoever did this to this girl made these or had them made."

"Do you have any fingerprints in the church?"

Joan made a face. "Unfortunately someone hadn't dusted the pews in a while. There are a million fingerprints in this place. It will take me years just to process all of them. I have nothing around the altar worth looking at. I'll dust and fog the place and check to see if anything interesting shows up. The carpet does show that the body was brought in through the back." She pointed to the carpet leading off to the back hallway. "You can see one set of footprints, and they indicated they were made by one person dragging the body. The back hallway leads to a side door opening out to an alley. I'm finished processing that area of the scene if you want to go down and take a look."

David went down the hallway to the side entrance. He opened the door and looked out into the alley. The gravel road was dry, with no sign of tire tracks. He looked across the alley to the rectory house. The nearest home next to the church was about half a block away across an open lot. There had been no moon last night, and the weather had been cloudy. He would have to interview the neighbors as well as the other people on the street to see if anyone had seen any unusual traffic last night. He sighed and went back into the church.

He went into the sanctuary and looked at the tile floor covered with dried blood. Joan came up to him. "There's a lot of blood and body fluids on the floor, as you can see. It's amazing that EMS got here in time to get her to the hospital."

She shook her head in disbelief. "I have a kid who looks like this girl, Dave. She was married in this church a few months ago," Joan said with a slight quiver in her voice. "I know we're not supposed to get emotionally involved, but this murder scares me. I hope we get this guy."

"I know Joan," David replied. "It's hard for me, too. This is not my favorite place in town right now. Who called 911?"

"A local paperboy saw the door of the church open while he was delivering papers. He went in, saw McKendrick on the floor and ran to a gas station and called in.

I've got his name and address for you."

"Thanks Joan. I'm going to the hospital to see McKendrick. Let me know if you find anything else." He started to leave, but Joan stopped him.

"Hey, cowboy, you take care of yourself, okay?" She gave him a brief hug. "You know we all care about you, right?"

"Yeah, Joan, I know. I just hope I can live up to what you all expect of me. I'll see you later." David's eyes were flooding with tears as he quickly walked away from her.

Joan watched him go out of the church. She looked down at the blood, and then at the toppled cross lying across the pews. *Lord, please send him something or someone he can hold onto. He's dying, and he needs your help,* she prayed silently as she got back to work.

David left the church through the front door and walked to his car. He knew that Joan was very careful, and very thorough. The initial crime scene report would be typed and on his desk by the end of the day, and all the samples would be on their way to the State Forensic Lab for additional processing and analysis. Compton's police force was small, but it was run by professionals, he thought to himself as he opened up the car's door.

His cell phone beeped. It was Carl. "Dave, are you still at the church?"

"I was just leaving. What's up?"

"Apparently Jenny Thatcher called her parents last night telling them she was on her way home from the rectory house. We contacted her parents this morning, and they told me that

McKendrick had given her money for a ticket to Albany. They're coming in later this morning to positively identify her body. I'd like you to be at the station when they arrive."

"Sure thing, Carl. I was about to go to the hospital to see if I could talk to McKendrick.

"Go ahead. I'll call you when they get in."

David hung up and drove down to the hospital that was located on Main Street. He went up to the ICU on the third floor. As he got off of the elevator, he could see that it was a very busy place. He could hear the sounds of beeping monitors and the low voices of doctors and nurses as they discussed various patients and their conditions.

Stepping up to the nurse's station, he showed his ID to one of the clerks. "I'm Detective Stone. Who is the nurse taking care of Angus McKendrick? I need to find out if it's possible for me to ask him some questions."

The clerk gave him with a strange look. "Stacey Michaels had Mr. McKendrick at the beginning of the shift this morning. She...well... She's down in the ER being seen right now. There was... an accident this morning."

"Accident?" David raised his eyebrows. "What kind of accident?"

"Why don't you head on down to the ER, Detective Stone? They'll tell you what happened down there. I'll page the supervisor and she'll meet you down at the ER."

"Thanks." David walked back to the elevator and went to the ground floor to the ER. He asked one of the receptionists where he could find Stacey Michaels.

The doctor had just finished putting in the final suture when David walked through the door of the treatment room. Stacey was obviously not happy about being there, and was gingerly holding a bag of ice next to her head.

"Ms. Michaels? I'm Detective Stone," David started out pleasantly, "I understand you were taking care of Father McKendrick when he was admitted to the ICU this morning."

"That's right, Detective," Stacey replied. "He arrived on our floor at around eight this morning. He had an MI, a heart attack, but he was stable when he got to our floor. About an hour ago, something…happened in his room, and he got much worse. That's when I passed out."

"What happened?"

Stacey suddenly became very quiet. "Doctor could you give us a moment alone, please?" she said in a low voice, looking at the doctor. He nodded slightly and left the room. David closed the door behind him.

Stacey looked at him apprehensively. "Detective, I want you to know that I've worked as an ICU nurse for ten years. I don't do drugs, alcohol, or anything else illegal. I'll be happy to take any kind of drug test, lie detector test, or anything else you want me to do. I've just finished a head CT, and I think they've taken about six quarts of blood from me to run every sort of test imaginable. Everything is dead normal, okay?"

David was puzzled. "Why are you telling me all of this?"

Stacey gestured impatiently. "Because what I'm about to tell you really happened. It couldn't have happened, but it did."

David sat down in a chair next to the stretcher where Stacey was seated. "I believe you, Stacey. Just go ahead with your story. Do you mind if I record this conversation?" He got out a pocket tape recorder.

Stacey relaxed. "Not at all," she said wryly, "It'll make a great Halloween yarn for our party this year." She laughed. "Father McKendrick came up at around eight, and I'd gotten him settled in bed and connected to all of the monitors and pumps. He's in good shape for an eighty-year-old man, and his heart attack didn't seem that major.

"About half an hour after he'd gotten to the unit, I noticed someone in his room. This guy was wearing a white coat, and I thought it was the cardiologist, so I didn't think anything of it. Five minutes later, Father McKendrick's alarms started going off. His blood pressure had suddenly dropped and he'd gone into a very slow dangerous heart rhythm. I went into his room, and there's this guy standing over McKendrick, whispering something to him in some language. I think it was German, but I'm not sure. Anyway, I yelled at him to get away from my patient. He turned around and gave me this horrible look."

"Do you have any idea who he was, or what he was doing there?" asked David.

Stacey looked at him. "No I don't. You see at that point, he walked out of the room. That's when I passed out."

"Did anyone see where he went?"

Stacey's voice dropped to a whisper, and she looked furtively around. "Detective, he didn't walk out the door. He walked through a wall. I know that sounds crazy, but that's what happened. No one saw him leave that room, Detective, no one."

There was a knock at the door. Stacey started violently and turned pale. The ER doctor came in, along with the nursing supervisor. "Stacey, you're going home for the rest of the day," the doctor said.

"But..."

"But me no 'buts', Stacey," the supervisor said. "Your patient is doing fine, and you need some rest." She softened her statement with a gentle smile at Stacey, who half-smiled back. "You'll be back tomorrow."

David waited until the doctor and Stacey had left the room before he spoke to the supervisor. "She's a good worker?"

"The best," the nursing supervisor replied in a tone that left no room for any objections to her assessment. "I wish I could figure out a way to clone her or something. She's one of the best nurses in the whole hospital."

"Is there any reason you could think of that might cause her to..."

"To what, Detective?" the supervisor asked sharply. "Make up an insane story like that? Absolutely not. Stacey's already told me what she saw. I believe her. I know what she told you sounds fantastic, but she isn't the sort to make thinks up."

"Well, I appreciate your opinion," David said. He moved towards the door. The supervisor stopped him before he left.

"Two more things, Detective," she said softly. "Father McKendrick is a wonderful man. Something evil happened to him in that church, and I think it's out to get him personally. You need to be careful."

David smiled. "Thanks for the warning. Is there a chance that I could see Father McKendrick sometime later today?"

"You'll have to talk to his physician about that. I'll try to arrange for that to happen. Doctors are sometimes hard to track down. Now if you'll excuse me, I have a hospital to run."

"Okay," David said, "Thanks again for your help."

James Rosson, Special Officer for Criminal Affairs at the British Consulate in New York, had a secret passion. He enjoyed reading the crime page of the *Post,* with all of its lurid sensationalism. As a senior diplomat at the Consulate, he felt bad about this, and took special care to conceal this information from his rather straitlaced colleagues. He felt that no one knew about this, or that he had developed a special relationship with the crime page editor. His wife found the situation hilarious and had frequently threatened to "out" him at times. He had had to buy her silence over the years with various rather expensive gifts.

James and the *Post* editor had traded tidbits of information as needed. They occasionally met at a local coffee shop at lunchtime, and generally the editor would call at around ten in the morning to set these meetings up. James' phone rang at ten this morning, and it was the crime desk editor at the other end of the line.

"Hello, Sidney. What kind of mayhem do you have for me this morning?" James greeted his friend.

"Jimmy, you're never going to believe what happened this morning," the editor started, speaking in a rapid-fire voice. "Some nut case set me a box full of guts to my office."

James didn't miss a beat. "Do tell," he said calmly. "One of your clients, I presume?"

"What are you talking about?" the editor yelled back. "Some lunatic mailed me a box full of human organs, and you want to joke about it? This is for real, okay?"

"All right, James said in a conciliatory tone. "Why are you telling me about this?"

"Because the nut case sent a note with the mess. I copied it before the Forensic guys arrived, and I want to send it to you. This guy signed it 'Jack the Ripper.'"

James chortled. "Yes, well, that makes everything different. I can certainly use another Ripper letter. I can add it to my burgeoning collection. I'll tell you what: I'll buy you a month's round of coffee if it's any good."

"You're on, pal," the editor replied. "It'll be coming over your fax shortly."

He hung up, and James turned on his fax machine. The machine lurched to life, stuttered and whirred in a busy fashion, and produced a thin sheet of paper. James reached over and took the page. His smile quickly faded as he read the note. Grabbing the paper in one hand, he swiftly dialed a secure transatlantic phone number.

"Hello? Yes, I need to speak with Charlie Warren... Hello, Charlie? Yes, this is James. Look, I'm relaying a fax sent to me this morning. Is there a chance that Bramshill could let you go for a few weeks? What? Well, take a look at it and see what you think. Goodbye."

He hung up the phone, only to have it immediately ring again. It was his assistant.

"Sir, the Consul wants to talk to you in her office."

"Tell her I'll be there right away," James stood up and buttoned his coat. The Consul's office was down the hall from his. Lady Margaret Wilson looked up as James walked through the door. She motioned James to take a seat.

"Father Angus McKendrick was involved in a murder that happened at his church in Compton last night. The New York Police Department phoned me about it a few moments ago."

The news shocked James Rosson. "Is he all right?"

"Well, he discovered the body in his church, and suffered some sort of heart attack. He's in their local hospital now. That's all I know at this time."

"Does Charlie Warren know about this?"

"No, not yet," Lady Margaret said enigmatically. "I need you to focus in on the facts right now, James. We will deal with personal issues later. The police also said that someone sent a letter to your friend over at the *Post* signing it 'Jack the Ripper' along with some of the murder victim's viscera."

James started at the mention of the *Post*. "Relax, James," she said in a motherly tone. "Your secret is safe with me, and Jane," she added wickedly with a glint in her eye.

Rosson decided to come clean. "I do speak to the crime editor at the *Post* on a regular basis, ma'am," he said. "In fact, he had just faxed a note to me before you summoned me to your office. Here it is." James handed it to Lady Margaret, who read it slowly and carefully before putting it down.

"Are you sure this is genuine?" she asked quietly. "Not one of those beastly jokes the Americans are so fond of playing on each other?"

"Yes ma'am, I am convinced it is genuine," Rosson replied. "I have seen the actual letters. This note is written in the same hand, and it mentions Warren's name."

"Yes, well, we need to look into this," the Consul said in her most business-like tone. "I take it you've already contacted Warren at Bramshill concerning the note?"

"Yes, ma'am, I have," James replied rather sheepishly. "I know I violated procedure by not clearing it with you first. Charlie Warren's a personal friend, you know."

"I understand, James. Charlie is a friend of mine as well," the Consul replied quietly. "You will make arrangements to have Dr. Warren over here to assist on the case as soon as possible. Do not tell Warren about Father McKendrick yet. This is not the sort of news you give to someone over a telephone line."

"Of course, thank you, ma'am." James left the office. The Consul frowned as she re-read the letter. It was horrifying, especially the last sentence:

Tell Charlie Warren I'm waiting

Jenny Thatcher's parents arrived at the police station shortly after noon. They were in Carl's office when David arrived. They had the shocked, scared look that parents get when horrible news comes to them about a beloved child.

David shook their hands. "I'm so very sorry about all of this," he glanced at Carl. "We need to have you come down to the Medical Examiner's Office to positively identify Jenny's body."

"Of course, Detective," John Thatcher said quietly, with a slight quiver in his voice. "We understand that this is necessary." David motioned them out the door.

The drive to the Medical Examiner's office was mercifully short. Carl had arranged for the Police Chaplain to meet them there at the viewing room. Jenny Thatcher's lifeless body was rolled up to the window, and the attendant lifted the drape from her face.

John gasped and Mary swayed for a second. "Yes, that's her," he finally croaked, his face streaming with tears. "How… Why did this happen to her?" he asked David. Mary was sobbing quietly in his arms as he steadied her.

David watched them, his own face working with his own remembered grief as they cried. "I don't know, Mr. Thatcher," he finally replied, his own voice choking with emotion. "But I can promise you that we are working very, very hard on finding out who did this to your daughter." The Chaplain gently took them out of the viewing room, and David was left alone for a moment. Watching them identify Jenny's body had brought back all of the awful memories of Karen's death: the funeral home, the endless line of mourners, and the final, awful moments at the cemetery as the casket closed on her pale face forever.

How am I going to be able to do this job again? He thought. David felt as though his guts had just been ripped out of his body. Suddenly his cell phone beeped and called him back to reality.

It was Carl. "NYPD just called. Their ME's got our missing girl's guts. It seems that the clown who did this sent them to the crime editor at the *Post* this morning as a joke."

"Well that's just great, Carl," David snarled back. "If you'd called a few seconds sooner I could have told the Thatchers the happy news personally."

"Hold on, Ace," Carl said. "I know that it's rough to take families to that room. Just get a grip on yourself, okay? Have you talked to the Medical Examiner yet?"

"No, I was saving that special treat for the end of the day," David replied sarcastically. "You know how much I love dealing with him."

"I know, Dave. Have the Chaplain drive the Thatchers back to the station. I'll handle them. You take the rest of the day off, understand?"

"But…"

"That's an order. If I see you down at the station before eight tomorrow, or hear of you snooping around the crime scene, I'll arrest you. Besides, you're coming over tonight and have supper with my family and me. That's an order, too, from my Boss."

"Yes, Master," David laughingly replied. "I'll see you later tonight." He turned off the phone. As long as he had friends like Carl, he could make it through his life. The empty hole where Karen had been was always with him, but at least people like Carl and his family made things better.

Angus McKendrick's body lay in the ICU, but his mind was back in the War. He could still hear the retreating whine of the Mosquito bombers that had unloaded his team over their target. His chute was floating down towards a camp lit by flames coming up from a hundred open furnaces. The thermal currents pushed his parachute away from his friends, away from the drop zone. He tried frantically to pull on the risers of his parachute to slip away from the ever-growing camp, but it was no use. Below, he could see the open maws of the furnaces, fueled by lifeless bodies dumped into them by skeletal beings. It was a scene from Dante's Inferno.

The ground rushed up as he prepared to land. He misjudged and landed hard, breaking his ankles on impact. A group of hideous figures surrounded him, more out of curiosity than fear. They parted quickly to make way for the guards of their prison who quickly took away his rifle.

Then he saw him. The man from his church; the one who had visited him in the hospital. His remorseless eyes bored into Angus, extinguishing all hope. Angus was going to die, slowly, hideously at the hands of this man and his minions. He groped for his pistol, not to defend himself, but to end his life. His hand was crushed by his captor's jackboot. Angus was hauled to his feet and forced to look into the impassive face of his tormentor.

"You think you have escaped, worm, but you have not. I will destroy you and all of the people you love," He croaked in

broken English. *"You cannot escape me, and I will come for you again."*

Suddenly the hideous scene was bathed in a bright light, and the evil form shrank back as though struck. Angus, now freed of his captors grasp, fell to his knees. He felt, rather than saw, someone come between him and the person who wanted to destroy him.

Angus turned his face upward to see his rescuer, but he saw only light. He heard his name being called, and opening his eyes, he found himself in his bed, alive and safe. The light distilled itself into bars of late summer morning streaming through his hospital window.

"I thought I was... somewhere else." Angus said weakly to his nurse, Stacey Michaels. She rewarded him with a bright, caring smile.

"Sorry, Father McKendrick, but you're still in the ICU, and you have me to deal with," Stacey said brightly. "The good news is that if all of your tests come out okay today, you'll be home today."

"That's good news, lass," Angus said, propping himself up on one elbow. "I have a sermon to write for Sunday and my garden needs mulching."

Stacey laughed merrily. "You'll have to wait for a little while, Father. Besides that garden of yours is so well tended, I'm sure it will survive for a few days without you."

"You miss the point, lass," McKendrick replied. "It's not the garden that's pining away, it's me."

"Father, who was that in your room yesterday? Did you see him?" Stacey's smile faded and her voice suddenly lowered itself down to a conspiratorial whisper. Angus looked at her for a moment, trying to measure his words.

"Aye lass, I saw him." he finally said, "and I can tell you that you were not dreaming when you saw what he did. I don't think he'll be back around here for a wee bit, though."

"Was it... he... a ghost?"

Angus smiled thinly. "No, lassie: he wasn't a ghost. Would to God he was, but he was no ghost."

"Then what...?"

"Stacey, my child, all you need to know right now is that he will not be back. You can trust me. He's not interested in you, and he won't be able to get back in here again."

Stacey gestured out to the police guard at the door of the room. "I can see that now."

Angus decided that the subject had gone on far enough. "Yes, love, that's right."

2

David slept past the alarm that morning. Carl finally called him up on the phone.

"Hello, is this Detective David Stone who *used* to work at the Compton Police Department? The *late* David Stone?"

"Wise guy," groaned David back into the phone. "What are you feeding your kids, Champ? They nearly beat me to death last night with all of those rides on my back."

"Oh, they just miss their favorite uncle, that's all," said Carl. "Listen, I need you to get in here as soon as you can. I just got some news about the Thatcher case."

"All right, I'm on my way." David reached over and looked at the clock: eight-thirty. He hadn't slept that late in months.

After a quick shower and a cup of really terrible leftover coffee, David drove down to the station.

Carl met him at his office door. He had a very strange smile on his face. David had seen the look before and knew immediately something was up.

"All right, mastermind, what are you scheming about now?" David warily asked, eyeing his friend watchfully.

Oh nothing, Dave, nothing at all," Carl replied, oozing with fake cheer. "It seems that our little murder has attracted some high-powered attention. I just got off the phone with the State Department. The British Consulate wants to send over some people to help us on the case."

"Help us? What does that mean? Why do we need 'their help'?" David asked in a puzzled tone. "The murder's barely forty-eight hours old. We've just gotten started."

"Here's the deal, Dave," Carl explained. "New York called up this morning. The guy who mailed the package with those organs sent a note with them and signed it 'Jack the Ripper'. So far, that's pretty typical. They get nut cases and Ripper notes by the truckload all the time. This note's different, because the handwriting matches some hundred year old samples of the Ripper's handwriting. The problem is that it's written on modern paper with modern ink. It also mentions the name of a British national named Charlie Warren."

David was not impressed. "So we have a nut case with a thing for the Ripper and he manages to computer-generate handwriting that looks like the Ripper's. Big deal."

"You aren't listening, Ace. The note's written by hand, and anyway, that doesn't matter right now. The bottom line is that we are going to have some help from the Brits on this case. That's it, okay?"

"So now what are we supposed to do? Wait for this expert from England to show up at high tea?"

Carl fixed his friend with a withering glance. "I happen to know Charlie Warren from the FBI Academy. Charlie's very bright, and very tough: someone you might learn from, Ace. You are going to the airport and pick up Charlie Warren this afternoon." Carl pulled out a sign labeled "Charlie Warren." Go to the British Airways section of the International Terminal with this sign and wait. Look for a fat little Englishman with red hair and a big mustache. That's Charlie."

"Why do I get the distinct impression I'm being set up?" David asked, taking the sign gingerly as though it would bite him.

"Because you are, but I'm still your boss, so get out of here now." growled Carl in a friendly way. "Charlie's a great guy. You two are going to get along just fine."

"I feel like a complete idiot," David thought. He was standing in the middle of the busy airport concourse with the sign "Charlie Warren" in his hands. Short dumpy Englishman with bright red hair and a big mustache: that was the description Carl gave to him. So far, no one even remotely fit the description. The plane was emptying out, and David started wondering if Carl had gotten the flight mixed up.

"Excuse me, sir, are you looking for Charlie Warren?" a low female voice said. David whirled around, nearly knocking the speaker off of her feet. He came to face with a petite young woman who was definitely not dumpy and had no trace of a mustache. His jaw dropped open for a moment. "I beg your pardon," he stammered, "Are you... Charlie Warren?"

"Yes I am," she replied. "Carl sent you, right? Let me guess: short dumpy Englishman with red hair and a mustache, or something like that."

"Yeah, that's what he said," growled David. "I'll kill him after I finish taking you to the hotel." Then he smiled.

It was hard not to smile around Charlie Warren. She did have red hair, but that is where Carl's description of her stopped being accurate. Charlie had beautiful golden auburn hair, along with a slightly upturned nose and a splash of freckles across her face. Her large eyes were deep green, almost emerald in color. They twinkled with laughter and amusement as she smiled openly at David. She looked like she had just finished high school.

Charlene Warren, M.D., Ph.D. also seemed to have an ability to read minds. "Carl and I met when I was lecturing at the FBI Academy. We're old friends. He told me a lot about you, David, and about the case. I'm looking forward to working with you. Let's get through Customs, okay?" She picked up her carryon bag, which was almost as big as her, and started off down the concourse at a breakneck clip.

After about five minutes, David had decided that Charlie Warren was also a good deal stronger than she looked, and was probably some sort of runner. "It's just up this rise," he puffed as they rounded a corner. A very tall, very thin man in a dark suit met them at the desk. Charlie put down her bag and practically knocked the man down with a hug.

"James!" she cried, "It's so good to see you! How are things going at the Consulate? How are Jane and the kids?"

James Rosson disengaged himself from Charlie's embrace. "They're all fine, Charlie. He turned to David. "I'm James Rosson, special assistant for Criminal Investigations. I work at the Consulate in New York. I've been sent to get this young lady through Customs."

David looked at this very friendly, non-traditional English greeting. "Looks like another stereotype of mine just bit the dust."

James laughed. "Yes, Charlie's definitely not your typical English girl famed in story and legend." He looked down at her with affection. She wrinkled her nose in reply. "It has to do with her mixed parentage."

"My mum was from Wales," explained Charlie. "Welsh women are... a little witchy. A bit magical, you might say."

"I'll keep that in mind," David said. He was starting to like this detective from England who was so very un-stuffy. The deep cloak of sadness, which had been hanging on him for the past three months, was starting to lift, ever so slightly.

"Consider yourself warned," James said, smiling slightly, noting David's reaction to Charlie with deep amusement.

He looked vaguely familiar to David. "Excuse me," David asked. "Were you ever over in the Gulf during the last war?"

Rosson's face brightened briefly. "Yes, I was. I worked with some of your chaps over there doing things we shouldn't talk about in public places. I believe I remember you from that area of the world as well. Fifth Group, wasn't it?"

"Yes," David said. "I remember you from a few of those situations. Glad to know Charlie runs around with the right crowd."

"You have no idea, Detective, of the sort of person you're dealing with," James said brightly. "Charlie Warren is an absolute menace and world-class troublemaker. Comes from a long line of cutthroats and pirates, Charlie does. Her ancestors sailed with Drake, and other renegades. The list of things her people have blown up is at least a mile long at last count..." his discourse was interrupted by a playful punch on his arm by Charlie.

"Stop it, James: you're scaring Detective Stone. Let's get this over with so we can get down to business. You can tell more lies some other time."

They finished up with the processing in a few short minutes, thanks to James' intervention. David was about to take Charlie to his car when James mentioned that Charlie had to stop by the Consulate for a few moments.

"I'm afraid we have a few more items to discuss with Dr. Warren before we release her into your care," Rosson explained. "She can pick up one of our cars and drive down to your station after she's done." Charlie shot him a knowing glance, and he nodded slightly.

"Do you know how to get to Compton?" David asked. "I could follow you over if you need me to."

"That won't be necessary, Detective Stone," Charlie replied. "I think I can find my way over to your station." She picked up her bag, and with Rosson in tow, sped away from the Customs counter.

David watched her go. Now that Charlie had left the area, the resentment he felt towards Carl welled up. He snatched his phone out of his coat pocket and dialed Carl. "Okay Slick," he snarled, "Your short dumpy Englishman arrived here safely. Some guy from the British Consulate picked her up. So now what do I do, besides come back to the station and beat you to death with this sign you gave me?"

"What's wrong, Dave? Didn't I give you the right information?"

"Let me see: wrong gender, wrong description. She does have red hair, but she comes up to my chin and she looks like she's about eighteen." David roared into the phone. People in the concourse were starting to stare at him and move away.

The phone made strangled laughing noises, which did nothing to improve David's mood. "Laugh it up, big guy. I'll deal with you later." He was tempted to throw the phone into a nearby trashcan.

Carl finally caught his breath. "Look, David, I had no idea that Rosson was going to pick her up. They didn't tell me that. But I'm not surprised, and besides, you needed something to shake you up a bit, okay?"

"All right," David grumped. "So now I'm down here in the city having wasted a trip to pick up a definitely not-fat, not mustache-wearing expert from England. Is she really a forensic expert, or is she some sort of English cheerleader? What next, sahib?"

"Head on over to the City Medical Examiner's office and pick up the report on the guts that got mailed to the *Post*. Also, you might want to swing by the *Post* and talk to the crime desk editor, since you're downtown. By the way, McKendrick has been released from the hospital this afternoon. You both can interview him tomorrow and hit the Medical Examiner's office. And yes, Dave, Charlie's the real deal, trust me."

"Thanks, buddy," growled David, "my life is complete. I'll deal with you when I get back to the office."

His mood failed to improve while he ran his errands in New York City. The package at the *Post* had caused most of the building to be evacuated for the better part of the day. The crime page editor was now receiving packages of garbage, animal entrails, and other noxious items through the mail from copycats. Interviewing Sid had not been a pleasant task. Print garbage, you get garbage, David decided as he left the building, which now had a separate area for handling obnoxious packages sent to Mr. Drucker.

He picked up the report from the City Medical Examiner's office on his way out of town. The two-hour wait at that office, coupled with the hour-long traffic jam out of the city, overheated David's car and his temper.

Both he and his ancient car were steaming when he pulled into the station parking lot. He saw that Charlie Warren had already arrived, noting the diplomatic plates on a black Nissan parked in the "Visitor" spot. She was already talking to Carl when David came into the office. They were discussing the note that had been sent along with Jenny Thatcher's organs to the newspaper.

"Well, while you two have been busy catching up on family news," David remarked sourly, "I've had a splendid time listening to a whiny weasel complain about getting nasty packages in the mail."

"Cool down, Dave," soothed Carl, "Charlie came in about two minutes before you did. She was just showing me this note everyone's so interested in."

"Well, go on, Dr. Warren, enlighten us poor Yanks on this lovely note," David said sarcastically.

His tone finally set Carl off. "Detective Stone, Dr. Charlene Warren is a noted expert in forensic science, both here and in the

United Kingdom. She is not only a personal friend of mine, but she is also here at the requests of the State Department and the British government. You *will* respect both her and her opinions, and you *will* cooperate with her fully. Is that clear?"

Carl's tone left no room for argument. Charlie had done nothing to deserve David's treatment of her. David felt suddenly embarrassed and ashamed. "I am really sorry I said those things. Please accept my apology."

Charlie rewarded him with a sweet, genuine smile. "That's all right, Detective Stone," she said graciously, "I know this is a very confusing and puzzling case, and I'm here to help in any way I can." David felt the warmth and kindness in her words. Smiling slightly, he sat down in a chair next to hers.

"You were just explaining to me about the note, Charlie, when David came in," Carl said. "You said that the note matches the correspondence that Scotland Yard received from the Ripper. I thought those letters were fakes."

"That's correct," Charlie replied, "the letters the public and most of the writers are familiar with are fakes. However, there is a body of correspondence from the Ripper to Scotland Yard that has been kept secret from the public. The handwriting on those letters and this note is an exact match."

David broke in. "How is it possible that the handwriting on a note written only a few days ago could exactly match correspondence received by Scotland Yard over a hundred years ago?"

"The obvious conclusion is that the note was written by the same person," Charlie said quietly.

David was incredulous. "No, that's not so obvious. Human beings don't live longer than a hundred years generally. How can that be possible?"

He turned to Carl. "Look Carl, we have a dead girl on our hands, two grieving parents who want to give their dead child a decent burial, and a case that's just gone into some sort of twilight zone of fairy tale nonsense. We need to find some sort of reasonable explanation for all of this, and quickly. You know how much the press loves this kind of stuff. They'll turn it into a media circus faster than you can blink your eyes."

"I agree with Detective Stone's assessment," Charlie said, "Whoever killed that girl is flesh and blood. We need to focus in on those elements now, and not the side issues. Do you have the Medical Examiner's report on Jenny Thatcher's body?"

"I have the report from the City ME's office, not our local branch," David replied. "I was hoping to get down there today, but I got rather busy in the City, as you both know."

"That reminds me, Dave, you got a call from 'ET' this afternoon." Carl said with a wry face. "His Majesty was none too happy that you weren't around waiting for his call with baited breath."

"Well some of us have lives and jobs to do without worrying about what flyweights like him are interested in," growled David.

Charlie looked at him quizzically. "'ET'? You get phone calls from aliens?"

"'ET' is shorthand for 'Evil Twin'" David explained. "My twin brother Bryan happens to run the district Medical Examiner's office. He's brilliant, thorough, and a complete jerk to deal with on a personal level."

"I see, no love lost here," Charlie observed. "Well, brotherly love or not, we need to get down there and talk to him. Perhaps I can assist on the examination of the body."

"I already checked with Bryan about that." Carl said. "He plans on doing the autopsy tomorrow. He'd like you and David to be there, first thing in the morning. I told him you'd be there."

"Thanks Boss," David grumped. "Any other news of note today?"

Carl looked at his watch. "Yeah, it's time to go home, Dave. I understand that Charlie has some loose ends to still tie up at the Consulate, so I'll see both of you tomorrow at eight. And Dave, try to make it on time, okay?"

"Okay, Boss. I need to get ready for tomorrow. Dealing with my brother requires lots of preparation," David stood up from his chair and turned to Charlie, "I'm really sorry about what I said earlier. I'm looking forward to working with you."

Charlie stood up and offered David her hand. "I am too, Detective," she said brightly. "We'll solve this little puzzle together." She turned and walked out the door.

David watched her go, and then he turned around and looked at Carl. "Is she really as good as you say she is?"

"Charlie Warren's the best in the business, Dave," replied his friend. "What's more, that note contains a personal threat to her. She's over here to find out why. I think you two are going to work well together, and don't be fooled by her sunny disposition. There's a lot going on in her life as well."

"Thanks for the tip, Carl. I'll see you tomorrow." David said as he left the office.

3

David did not sleep past his alarm the following morning, but for the first time in months since Karen died, his sleep was untroubled by bad dreams. He woke to the sound of his phone ringing. Reaching over to the bedside stand where the phone was, he noticed the time on the clock: five-thirty.

"Please leave your name and address so I can come over and kill you later," David said, clutching the phone in a close approximation of the technique he planned on using on the caller's throat.

"What a wonderful way to say 'hello', Detective," chirped an obviously wide-awake and exuberant Charlie Warren. "Would you like to join me in a little run before breakfast?"

David groaned. He knew it: Charlie's demonstration at the airport of her physical stamina was accurate. "Okay, Charlie," he finally said. "It'll take me a few minutes to get dressed and down to the hotel."

"Oh you needn't bother about the hotel, David. I ran down to your house and I'm right outside your door."

But...it's five miles from my house to the hotel." David stammered. "You ran five miles down to my house already? You don't even sound winded."

"Yes, it's a lovely day out here. Get ready and I'll be waiting." she hung up.

David looked at the phone as though it were a poisonous snake. He lurched out of bed and struggled into an old jogging suit. This was not going to be pretty.

When he was finished, he opened the door. Charlie Warren was there, dressed in a powder blue jogging suit. To David's immense disgust, he noted she was not even sweating.

It was a beautiful day. The air was cool and the early morning sunlight was glinting off of Charlie's hair in tones of gold-flecked copper. I'm going to die and this beautiful doctor is going to have to give me CPR, David thought as he smiled bleakly at her.

"Well, let's get started", she caroled, starting off at a brisk trot.

It was five miles of agony, as David's out-of-shape body told him every step of the way. Mercifully, Charlie kept a fairly slow pace, out of consideration for her older and very out-of-shape companion. Maybe it was having her around, or the fact that the day was cool and beautiful, but David actually felt better at the end of the jog to the hotel.

Charlie politely waited until David caught his breath. "There's a shop across the street where we can have some breakfast, if you'd like."

"Thanks," David puffed. "The ER's just down the block. We can call EMS and they can pick me up at the restaurant."

"Oh come on, David; that was just a little jog. You can't be that out of shape." She said, tugging at one of her shoes. "Let's go over to that little diner." Charlie pointed to a diner next to the hotel marked "Sophie's."

"Sure, why not? Every cop in town is there right now, having coffee and eating donuts. Wait a minute while I get out my gun so I can shoot myself when we're done." David moaned.

"It can't be all that bad," Charlie said playfully. I wish she wasn't so cute, David thought. It's impossible to be around her and not smile.

"Let's just go in and sit down, okay?" he finally whined, limping gingerly across the street. Sophie's Diner was a tradition in Compton. All the cops on the police force ate there because the food was good.

All eyes turned towards David and Charlie when they walked through the door. Charlie was the one who got most of the attention. They got a hearty helping of whistles and greetings before they finally sat down at a booth to order their food. David limped along behind Charlie, convinced that his life was finally over.

"Half the force is here in this place this morning, and the other half will know about this by noon today," he groaned.

"Relax, David, you'll survive, I promise you." Charlie said brightly, wrinkling her nose in a beguiling way. "I think you've needed to get out and do something like this for a long time."

David looked at her. "Yes, self-torture was definitely on my 'to do' list, along with public humiliation. Just what exactly did my bigmouthed boss tell you about me?"

Charlie looked at her coffee for a moment quietly before she answered. "Just that you'd lost your wife a few months ago, and that you've been having a bad spell at work, that's all. I can make some educated guesses about what you've been going through. I can promise you that I'm not going to pry."

David looked at her for a moment. The sympathy and compassion in her eyes was real. He smiled awkwardly at her. "I appreciate that, Charlie, and you're right. I got into the habit of feeling sorry for myself, and I've tried to pull the rest of the world down into my hole." He picked up the menu. "I really enjoyed the run, but now it's my turn. The omelet here is a death-dealer. Are you up for it?"

"Why not?" Charlie replied, "Who lives forever?"

"Great, because I'm buying you breakfast. I also need to ask you: did you run track in college?"

Charlie smiled at him. "No, nothing of the sort. I did get as far as the Olympic tryouts, though."

"Don't tell, me. Let me guess," David interrupted, trying to be creative. "Fencing and full-contact karate." He started eating his omelet. Charlie gave him a delighted smile.

"How ever did you guess?" This statement nearly produced a choking spell on the part of David.

"I must be reading minds," he croaked, once his airway was clear.

After they finished breakfast and paid for their meal, David got up from the table. The immediate spasms of pain in his legs told him that he had five miles between him and a hot shower.

Charlie read his mind. "Relax, David: I was planning on driving you back to your house."

"Thank you for your mercy, Charlie," David , limped painfully to the door. They got into the car and drove to David's house.

On their way to his house, David had the opportunity to study Charlie a little more closely. The sun played off of her shoulder-length hair, which framed her features nicely. Her deep green eyes stayed on the road, but suddenly they flicked over to him and caught him looking at her. She stuck out her tongue at him in an impish gesture that made her look adorable.

The gesture took David aback. "I thought English girls were supposed to be humorless, proper, and very uptight."

"Guess again," she said brightly. "Molds are made to be broken."

He got out of the car, and managed to walk fairly upright to the door. David turned around to wave and smile at Charlie as she pulled out of his driveway, then collapsed though the open door.

Thirty minutes later he was showered, dressed, and at the station. Charlie was there, waiting for him. She had brought along a small medical bag and was wearing a lab coat. David looked at her and raised his eyebrows.

"House call?" he asked.

Charlie looked up and smiled. "It helps sometimes to bring along a few props to impress the natives."

"No argument there," David said. "You'll need all of that and more to impress Bryan. A few framed medical degrees from some Ivy League schools would be in order."

"The schools I attended were turning out doctors when there was nothing in America but trees and red Indians," retorted Charlie.

"Ouch, that'll hurt. File that away and use it on him when he gets too big for his britches." Carl walked into the station. "Well, hello Boss. Alarm not go off today? I guess the kids pound on you when I'm not around."

Carl glowered at him. It was an open secret around the station that he loved roughhousing with his kids at home. "Let's can the comedy right now, okay? After you finish at the Medical Examiner's office, you can go by Trinity and interview McKendrick."

"Never fear, old chap," quipped David in a horrible British accent, "the intrepid team of Stone and Warren are on the case."

Charlie covered her ears. "David, that was absolutely horrible! What price do I have to pay you to never do that again?"

David gave her a lopsided grin. "I'll think of something later."

Carl groaned. "I think I've created a monster, pairing you two together."

"A proper two-headed one, I think," said Charlie gleefully.

"Get out of my police station, you two," snapped Carl, "Dave, go torture your brother for a while. Give him my love."

"As you wish, Sire," bowed David as they walked out the door. Turning to Charlie, he barked, "Watson, the game's afoot. To the hansom cab, and step on it!"

Carl watched them leave out the door, a smile playing across his face. He was very pleased on the way they interacted. They would work well as a team, and that was good for the solving of this case. Carl was secretly hoping that they would be good for each other as well. Charlie and David were very special people: people who deserved to be happy and whole. Perhaps they could find such happiness in each other.

Joan Richards, came up beside him and read what was going through his mind. "Chemistry," she said, and looked at him with raised eyebrows and a smile. "Who's the teenager with David? She's a little young for him, I think."

"That's Charlie Warren, the forensic investigator the Brits sent over to help with our case." Carl replied.

"That's Charlie Warren?" Joan was incredulous. "I've read some of her work. She looks younger than my teenage daughters. What did she do, go to college when she was in diapers?"

"Oxford University at fourteen, or something like that." Carl said absently. Being around Charlie befuddled him for some reason. Joan noted it with amusement.

"Well, she's really cute. David seems to think so, obviously. Things are going to be very interesting around this burg from now on," she predicted enigmatically.

"What are you talking about?" stuttered Carl, uncomfortable at being found out to have a sentimental streak (a trait so blindingly obvious to everyone who worked with him that no one ever commented about it).

"Oh, nothing. Nothing at all." Joan said blithely, handing him a report on the crime scene and shifting gears to all business in a microsecond. "The crime scene's been processed, and I've given clearance for the church people to clean the mess up at Trinity." I agree completely," said Carl, relieved to be talking about business again. "I wonder if I should warn 'ET' about what's headed his way." He thought about it for a moment, "Nah. Some things are just better enjoyed as surprises."

As he was speaking the "surprise" was pulling up to the Medical Examiner's office. David got out of the car and ran around to Charlie's door, graciously opening it.

"You drive very well for someone who's used to driving on the wrong side of the road, Madam." David bowed with a flourish.

"Wise guy," retorted Charlie, "I'll match my driving skills next to yours any day of the week, cowboy."

"Them's fightin' words in these here parts, missy," drawled David in a really bad Texas accent. They approached the door. "All right, it's time to put our game faces on.

After you, your grace," he said, opening the door for Charlie, who shot him a venomous look.

Bryan Stone was waiting for them in his office. Charlie observed that the two brothers were virtually identical, at least physically, but there the resemblance ended.

There was no warmth in Bryan's eyes, no humanity. His face had a set, heavy look that made his features appear as though they were made out of marble, and not flesh.

His voice had no animation either. "Come in, David. Your white-coated colleague must be Dr. Warren. I've heard of your work over in Britain. Please sit down."

After they were seated, Bryan handed them a sheet of paper listing his preliminary findings. "I've listed the cause of death as hypovolemic shock due to massive fluid loss. This conclusion is based on my initial assessment and not as the result of the autopsy. I presume that you wish to assist in the autopsy, Dr. Warren?"

"I am looking forward to it, Dr. Stone," replied Charlie in a professional, clinical tone that matched Bryan's inflection for inflection. "Have you been able to come up with a sequence of injury yet?"

"No, of course not," Bryan's voice, chilly to begin with, grew several degrees colder. "That determination cannot be made until the body is thoroughly examined. Would you care to follow me to the autopsy suite?"

He led them out of his office and down a long corridor to the autopsy suite. "You may want to change into scrubs before we examine the body." Bryan gestured to the door marked "Dressing Room." "You can find some scrubs in there."

By the time they had changed into scrubs, Jenny Thatcher's body was already out on the autopsy table. She looked frail and pathetic under the harsh florescent light. A great surge of pity welled up in David's heart for her, and for her parents. What had been done to this poor girl was an obscenity. Charlie glanced at him briefly and noted the pain in his face. David glanced over at her and she nodded slightly, acknowledging her agreement with his feelings.

"She certainly hadn't been eating much, lately," he observed, noting the wasted appearance of her body.

"Part of that is due to the fact that the murderer stripped away most of the subcutaneous fat as he was skinning her," observed Bryan with as much empathy as someone would have for a cockroach. "However, I do agree with your assessment."

"How kind of you to agree with me, Bryan," David shot back. "This is not one of your dissecting projects. Jenny was, and is a human being. She had parents who loved her and are grief stricken about her death. Try to keep that small fact in your mind."

Charlie noted the exchange. "Gentlemen, let's proceed with the external exam, shall we?" She moved around to the head, studying the mouth closely. The endotracheal tube which the medics had placed to ventilate her was still taped in place. "She was found hanging from a cross in the church, correct?"

"Yes, that's right," David answered.

"Well, she was on a ventilator prior to that," noted Charlie. "Her lips are displaced to the right side, and there is marked swelling around her mouth. She was intubated by the medics when they were trying to resuscitate her, but the extent of the swelling and mouth trauma indicates a prior endotracheal tube has been placed in her mouth."

"An arresting theory, Dr. Warren," observed Bryan. "Why do you think such a thing was done to the victim?"

"To control her airway while the murderer operated on her," replied Charlie grimly. Bending closer to Jenny's face, she studied her mouth. "There is a darker line of adhesive of a different sort framing Jenny's mouth, indicating at some point that her mouth was covered with a strip of wider tape, probably duct by the look of it. There is also some indication of bruise marks on the right side of her face, indicating that she was attacked from behind and her face and mouth were held while she was subdued."

Charlie moved down methodically to Jenny's neck. "There is an insertion site at the junction of the right sternocleidomastoid, indicating that someone inserted a large bore intravenous catheter, perhaps to monitor blood pressure and to instill medications and fluids. Additionally, there is a smaller puncture site inches below this with bruising noted. Something was injected into her at that point, probably with considerable force."

She walked around the table to look closely at Jenny's hands. "Even though the victim's skin was removed, I can see some banding marks around her wrists, indicating that at some point, her wrists were restrained."

Moving to the bottom of the table, Charlie looked at Jenny's ankles. "She was tied at the ankles as well, since there are banding marks around the ankles, though they are not nearly as prominent as the ones on her wrists."

Bryan was standing back, watching Charlie make her initial exam. "Fascinating performance, Dr. Warren." he finally said mockingly.

Charlie turned on him quickly. "Do you disagree with my findings so far, Dr. Stone? Is there something I may have overlooked?"

"No, of course not," replied Bryan in a tone which apparently was his attempt to soothe an injured ego. "It's just that you seem to be rapidly drawing conclusions before you have even finished your collection of data."

"I respectfully disagree with your opinion, Doctor," said Charlie in a tone with matched Bryan's for coldness. "Based on my experience with *ante mortem* trauma and wounding analysis, I believe that my conclusions are more than adequately based on solid evidence. Let us proceed to the examination of the marks of crucifixion."

Charlie went to Jenny's wrists and carefully lifted them up with her gloved hands. "The victim was crucified with nails which passed from the anterior wrist through the Point of Destot and secured her to the wood of the cross. The injures are *ante mortem* in nature, owing to the presence of swelling noted in the surrounding ligamentous tissues. You will note the classic abduction of the thumb which occurs when the median nerve is severed."

She examined Jenny's feet. "The victim's feet were nailed to the cross just above the union of the tibia and fibula with the bony foot."

Charlie stood up and looked at Bryan. "This woman was operated on, skinned alive, nailed on a cross in a church, and left there to die. She was killed by someone skilled in medical science who knew how to stabilize her long enough to torture her thoroughly in the most hideous fashion possible while keeping her alive in order to complete the operation."

"Aren't you jumping to conclusions, Doctor?" Bryan asked smugly. "I see no skill in the injuries inflicted on this woman. Anyone can skin a body; deer hunters do that sort of thing all the time."

"Indeed, that's true," Charlie shot back. "But the insertion of a large intravenous catheter in the neck indicates medical knowledge of fluid resuscitation and use of hemodynamic monitoring." She moved to the abdomen and reflected the flap of skin over the abdominal cavity. "I see evidence of an electrocautery device being used to provide hemostasis on the minor blood vessels." David and Bryan moved closer to the table to peer into the girl's now-empty abdominal cavity. "The great vessels have been expertly ligated, and the organs of the abdominal cavity have been removed as a whole, *en bloc*." Charlie paused briefly. "He was kind enough to leave the uterus and ovaries, as well as her kidneys."

"Do you have any speculation as to why those particular organs were spared, Doctor?" asked Bryan in an acid tone. Obviously he was tiring of this upstart doctor from Britain.

"I'll ask the killer when I find him," replied Charlie quietly. "I presume you had X-rays made of the body?"

"Yes, of course, we do have that technology here in the United States now, Dr. Warren," Bryan and Charlie walked over to the viewing board where some X-ray films were hanging. Charlie observed the films briefly.

"She didn't die from the complications of crucifixion, obviously," Charlie said matter-of-factly. "Judging from her chest x-ray, the shock and trauma of the fluid loss prevented her from going into congestive heart failure and asphyxiation, which are the primary causes of death from crucifixion. I see no evidence of any fractures to any bones or foreign objects inserted into the victim's body."

Charlie turned to Bryan. "The toxicology studies will be crucial in determining what drugs were used on her. My preliminary guess would be that she will have traces of short and long acting neuromuscular paralytics, as well as some short-acting benzodiazepines. You are planning to send off tissue specimens for analysis, aren't you?"

"Of course we are, Dr. Warren. Forensic medicine has attained some level of sophistication here in the colonies, you know. We haven't done that yet, of course, since we are still on the external exam of the body." Bryan said grimly and with finality. "I appreciate your input into this case, Doctor. Your performance today has been... remarkable."

Turning to his brother, he said. "And you, David: always a pleasure to see you. Now if you'll both excuse me, I need to conclude the autopsy. I believe you can show yourselves out." He turned away from them.

"Well thanks, Bryan, for all of your help." David said acidly. "We'll be waiting for your report." Bryan made no attempt to reply, busying himself with removal of the girl's heart and lungs. Charlie and David turned around and left the autopsy suite.

"What a wonderful way to spend a summer morning," observed David in the corridor as they were walking out the door. "Yes, he is human, even though he comes across as a robot. It's been a while since I've seen someone who could stand up to Bryan and give back to him some of the stuff he so liberally dishes out.

I'm impressed, Dr. Warren." David concluded in a complimentary fashion.

Charlie said nothing in response as they walked to the car. David kept wondering about this girl. It was hard to reconcile the picture of the brilliant medical professional he'd just seen in action with the laughing, engaging young woman he'd been having breakfast with two hours ago. There was much, much more to Charlene Warren than met the eye, David concluded.

He finally broke the silence after they had been driving for a few moments. "I think we have time to stop at Trinity before noon. Would you like to do that?"

Charlie smiled and relaxed. "Good, that sounds really good. I need to see Uncle Angus after all of that."

David's jaw dropped. "Uncle Angus? Are you related to him?"

"No, not really," said Charlie. "He's more like a very dear family friend. He was in the Second World War with Grandfather. Angus is really wonderful."

They arrived at Trinity to find Angus tending to his garden, and a cleaning truck pulled up to the front door of the church. As they got out of the car, David explained to Charlie that the crime scene had been already processed, and the church was being restored so that the people could worship there on Sunday.

"That's good," agreed Charlie. She ran over to Angus, who turned just in time to avoid being bowled over. "Uncle Angus!" she cried as she held onto him as though he would turn to water and slip away from her.

"Charlie, lass, it's good to see you again." Angus said brokenly through tears as he held her and stroked her hair. "Why, I haven't seen you since… since I was back in Britain a few months ago."

Charlie finally disengaged herself from Angus and introduced David. "Uncle Angus, this is Detective David Stone. He's investigating the death of Jenny Thatcher."

David moved forward and extended his hand. "A pleasure, sir. The last time we met was at my wife Karen's funeral."

"Oh yes, of course, I remember you now, David," a deep cloud of sadness passed over Angus' face. "Such a terrible tragedy, your wife's death." He shook his head, and then brightened up. "But here

I am forgetting my manners. Will you not come in and have some tea with me in the parlor? We can talk there uninterrupted."

Angus ushered them into the rectory parlor, which also doubled as his study. The room was filled with books and was rather dark. Angus had insisted on keeping his own house, much to the consternation of the more fastidious vestry members. David noted that a good many of the books were in Latin, Greek, and Hebrew. McKendrick was not a stellar housekeeper, but there was absolutely nothing wrong with his mind. The clutter bespoke extreme mental activity, not tumbled disorder.

After excavating two chairs from a stack of ponderous tomes. Angus bade his guests to sit down. After they were seated, he went off in search of the wherewithal to make tea. He clattered about noisily in his kitchen, humming tunelessly.

"Angus, you shouldn't be out there in the garden. You just had a heart attack." Charlie gently scolded him. Her remark caused the noise in the kitchen to get even louder than before.

"Can you think of a better place to die and meet God than in a garden surrounded by flowers, lass?" Angus' voice floated out of the kitchen over the din.

"You know what I'm talking about, Uncle Angus. Don't start getting theological with me. It doesn't work." Charlie shot back.

"Then don't start getting clinical with me, young lady." Angus responded quickly.

The exchange deeply amused David, who looked over to Charlie and raised his eyebrows. "How old is Father McKendrick?"

"Old enough now to where age and birthdays no longer matter," replied Charlie, slightly irritated. "I think he's around eighty or so. Yes, around eighty. Grandfather kept telling me how impressed he was that his team sergeant had almost finished seminary when Grandfather first met him. Angus came over to America after he finished his seminary training."

"I've been a bachelor ever since Forty-two, if the truth must be told," said Angus, coming back into the room and seamlessly joining into the conversation. "My Moira was a nurse in London during the Blitz. Unfortunately one night an errant Messerschmidt strafed her car as she was traveling home from working at Bart's. I was over in Libya at the time. I didn't hear about her death until some weeks later when I returned to the British lines."

Angus set the tea tray down in front of his two guests. "But enough of all this blathering on my part. I imagine you want to talk to me about the night that poor Jenny died."

"Yes sir, that's why we're here. Do you mind if I record your conversation?" David produced a small pocket tape recorder.

"No, of course, not at all," Angus said graciously, settling back into a chair with his tea.

"What time did Jenny Thatcher arrive here on Sunday?"

Angus thought for a moment. "Let me see. It was around eight-thirty or so. I had just closed up the church and had come over to the rectory to study for this Sunday's sermon when I heard a knock at the door. It was Jenny, and she looked terrible. The poor lass had not eaten anything in the last two days, and her clothes were in rags. She begged me to let her come in for a moment and get a drink of water. Naturally I did more than that. I let Jenny in, allowed her use of the bathroom to wash up a bit, found her some clothes that fit her in our church charity closet, and sat her down for a good meal. When she was through, I talked to her a bit, and convinced her to go home. I called the ticket office downtown, gave Jenny some money, and arranged for her to pick up a ticket for her to go back to Albany. She was really excited about meeting her parents. Since it was late, I called her a cab. One arrived about two minutes later, and that's the last I saw of her until... that morning."

Angus' voice became unsteady. "Jenny was a poor hungry child. What he did to her was horrible." He put his head in his hands for a moment.

"What time did the cab pick her up, Uncle Angus?" Charlie asked gently, holding one of his hands.

Angus looked at her for a moment. "Around nine-thirty, I think. You know, Charlie, she reminded me of you in some ways." He smiled at her. "Why are you over here in America, lass?"

"Somehow I've been threatened by the same killer that killed Jenny Thatcher, Uncle Angus," said Charlie, producing a copy of the letter sent to the *Post*. He sent this letter to a newspaper here in New York along with the poor girl's organs."

"May I see the letter?" asked McKendrick, producing a pair of wire-rimmed glasses. Charlie handed him the letter. He took it from her, and read it slowly. His hands started to tremble midway through the letter.

"You understand what this means, Charlie," Angus said finally, handing the letter back to her. "You are in terrible danger."

"Yes, Uncle Angus, I know that," Charlie said in a comforting tone. "You know I can take care of myself."

"Charlie, my dearest, you underestimate your opponent," Angus said, standing up and pacing the floor. "This is not a garden variety of criminal you are dealing with. You are facing something truly terrible: a monstrous evil who is immensely powerful and incredibly intelligent."

Charlie saw that Angus was getting more and more upset. "I think it's time for us to leave, Uncle Angus. I promise you I'll be back later on when we can visit some more."

"Yes, that sounds good, Charlie," Angus responded gratefully. "You and I need to have a very long talk about certain family matters. Don't brush me off, love, this is important."

"I promise, Uncle Angus, we'll be back, and I'm not brushing you off." Charlie stood up and hugged him. He kissed her cheek.

"Thank you, Father McKendrick, for your time." David stood up and held out his hand.

Angus took it, and looked him square in the eye. "You understand, lad, that Charlie is precious to me. She is the only family I have left this side of Heaven. Her life has been placed in your hands, and you are now accountable for that life."

"Yes sir," David said, strangely chastened by what Angus had said. "I'll try to look after her."

"That's a task daunting enough for a hundred of God's finest angels," laughed Angus, embracing Charlie again. "Take care, love."

David's cell phone rang as they were leaving the rectory. It was Carl: "Charlie needs to go over to the British Consulate and meet with James Rosson this afternoon. She can drop you off at the station."

"Fine," David responded, looking at Charlie. "I need some desk time to sort all of this stuff out." He hung up. "Looks like you have a delightful afternoon planned for you courtesy of your government."

Charlie grimaced. "More like bureaucratic water torture. I can't believe James actually likes his job." They arrived at the police station. "Well, here we are," she said brightly. "Home again in the same afternoon. Try to not get too bored while I'm away."

David got out of the car. "I'm counting the seconds," he said, closing the door. She drove off, leaving him staring after the rapidly receding car. He shook his head and went in through the station door. Strangely enough, he really *was* counting the seconds until she got back.

Everyone was standing and clapping as he came in. The desk sergeant ceremoniously handed David a beautifully wrapped gift. "The boys and I decided to give you a present in honor of seeing you this morning in that tacky jogging outfit and miserable shoes. Since you're running around with classy women now, you need to step up and dress better," she said, winking heavily in his direction. She reached over and kissed David on the cheek, confidentially whispering to him, "Seriously, everyone here is really happy for you."

He drew back, red in the face. "Well, thanks, I guess. I don't know what you're talking about." David opened the box: it was a pair of new running shoes. They were colored a venomous purple and putrid green. He smiled and bowed in the direction of the applause and cheers. "What? There's no matching beanie to go with the shoes? What a rip-off!" he said, rummaging around in the box.

David went over to his desk and the station settled down to work. Joan Richard's crime scene report was sitting on his desk, ready for his digesting. That task would take him the better part of the afternoon. David was a careful worker, and he didn't like to leave anything to chance. For the first time in months, David felt confident that he could handle a tough case and be able to solve it. He actually felt good about what he was doing. The gift from his friends was a playful reminder that they wanted him to be back on track as well.

While David was receiving his honors as a born-again track star, Charlie was busy driving into New York City to the British

51

Consulate. Her mind was working on several levels, as well as attempting to negotiate the usual trial of driving.

She thought about her encounter with Bryan Stone. He obviously had a tender ego when it came to his profession, and was not used to being challenged or questioned in any way. Charlie was used to that sort of thing. It was unfortunately a too-common phenomenon in the medical arena, especially among the practitioners of more esoteric fields such as forensic medicine. She decided that with a little diplomacy on her part, she could extract the needed amount of information from Dr. Stone with a minimum amount of trauma to his tender psyche. And women are the ones whose egos are fragile, she thought archly.

Bryan's relationship with David puzzled her. She was thoroughly familiar with the psychodynamics of sibling rivalry, but her own relationship with her brother was completely devoid of intense conflicts. It was foreign to her own experience.

The thought of her brother threatened to open a door into a world of sadness that she was not willing to enter at this time. She deliberately shifted her mind into thinking of Angus and what a joy it was to see him again. Charlie decided that she would take him out to dinner at the first opportunity and catch up with him. That thought brought a smile to her face, just as she pulled into the British Consulate parking area.

James was in his office, waiting for her. "A sunny day for a sunny girl," he said, kissing Charlie lightly on her cheek in greeting. "I'm sorry to tear you away from your work in Compton, but my superiors want me to grill you on how things are going."

Charlie looked puzzled, "Well, fine, for the first two days, I guess. It's really early to form any sort of opinions on how things are going. We've just gotten started."

"I know, I know," James held up a sympathetic hand, "I tried to explain that to them, but they insisted on having me drag you in here. If nothing else, to remind you that you're not on holiday over here. You should have heard the screams from Bramshill when they heard we were pulling you to send you over here to America."

Charlie made a face. "I can imagine how it sounded. Probably like the monkey house at the zoo."

James laughed. "That's a fair description of it. Your presence here seems to be generating screams on this side of the pond as well." He shuffled through a small stack of papers on his usually tidy desk, producing a phone record. "It seems that the local Medical Examiner called his superiors and told them that he didn't appreciate your appearance at his office this morning. Made a big to-do about having an unlicensed medical practitioner interfering with his investigation."

Charlie snorted. "That's ridiculous. Dr. Stone invited us to come back and observe the autopsy. We came at his request. I just simply gave him some of my professional opinions."

"I know what kind of professional opinions you give, young lady, and I know how well they are usually received. Not that they're wrong, but most professionals in your line of work are worse than movie stars when it comes to ego and temperament. Well, it's obvious that Dr. Stone did not appreciate your input." James observed wryly. "And as your 'superior', (and I use that term loosely) I have been instructed to let you know that you are to exercise more tact in dealing with our counterparts."

Charlie struck a demure pose. "I will be the model of discretion," she said sweetly. Her green eyes twinkled with amusement.

James roared with laughter. "Stop that, or I'll personally throw you out of this building! You are a complete pest, you know. It's amazing that I'm still sane with you and Jane in my life." He calmed down and changed the subject. "You saw Angus this morning. How is he doing?"

"He's fine," replied Charlie. "He's got the constitution of a horse, but he's going to get in trouble if he's not careful. Being eighty years old hasn't caught up with him...yet."

"Well, I'm glad he's doing better. By the way, Lady Margaret would like you and your detective friend to attend a little function on Saturday night. Are you interested?"

"Of course," said Charlie brightly. "I'd love to come. I'll have to ask David...I mean Detective Stone, if he'd like to come."

James sat back in his chair for a moment. "What do you think of him?"

Charlie looked back at him steadily. "Detective Stone is a fine investigator. I'm glad I'm working with him and his department. Compton may be a small town, but it has a fine police force."

"Evaded like a true expert," James said, boring in. "But you haven't answered the question, Doctor. Look, darling, I know you, so don't play coy with me. It doesn't work."

Charlie said softly. "It's too early for that sort of thing, James. You know what I've been through these past few months."

"Well in that case, off you go." said James cheerily. "Try not to upset the natives: it causes ever so much trouble."

"You know me, James: the model of diplomacy!" laughed Charlie in return.

"That's what I'm afraid of." James shot back. "See you on Saturday." He kissed her goodbye.

Charlie drove back to the Compton police station to find David at his desk buried under a mound of reports, holding his head. Obviously his efforts to organize the case had not gone well.

"My head hurts," David whined as Charlie breezed in through the station door.

"What's wrong? Things not adding up?" she asked cheerily, shuffling through one of the less tidy heaps on his desk.

"Not adding up? You must be joking." he replied glumly. "Sunday night must have been a wonderful night to sleep in this burg. No one seems to have seen or heard anything that night. I've interviewed every neighbor on the street where Trinity is located. Everyone said that it was completely quiet that night. Joan's crime scene report is very thorough, but we have no usable prints at the scene. The carpet and fiber samples have been sent off to the State Crime Lab. There are no dirt samples from her fingernails, because the killer thoughtfully removed her fingernails, along with the rest of her skin. Did I show you the nails this creep nailed her to the cross with?" David tossed an evidence bag containing the nails onto the desk. "These things are a complete mystery as well."

Charlie picked up the bag. "I know where they came from," she said quietly. "I saw nails like these once in Israel, at an archeological dig to be precise. They are nails of the sort that were common back in the first century. The Romans used them to crucify criminals." She shuddered as she said those words.

David stared at her. "So our victim was crucified by someone using two thousand year-old nails?" He shook his head. "Why would someone do that?"

Carl came up to the desk. "Trouble, children?" he asked lightly.

"We're just trying to make some sense of all this mess, and it's not happening." David responded. "So far we have a murdered girl who was killed on the most peaceful Sunday in Compton's history. There are no traces of the killer left at the scene, except for some antique nails from Israel."

"Well, you'll just have to sort all of that out tomorrow, because I'm sending you home for the day." Carl said firmly. He turned to Charlie. "David is not allowed to stay after school. Seventy-two hour weeks are bad for his health, and I am not going to have all of the progress he's made over the past few days undone at this point."

"Yes master," David mockingly said, getting up and putting on this coat. "Well, I'm off to my house for a quiet night of television and feasting on frozen pot pies."

Charlie made a horrible face. "That's disgusting, David. Why don't I take you to dinner?"

"Yes, why don't you take him to dinner?" chimed in Carl, obviously pleased at the prospect. "Charlie, David is the worst cook on the planet. He can burn water. His kitchen has been labeled by the EPA as a hazardous waste dump."

"Well then, it's settled. As a doctor, I'm under a sacred oath to preserve life, and saving David from filthy frozen pot pies definitely falls under those responsibilities." Charlie said firmly. "Do you have any suggestions, other than that diner we tried this morning?"

"There's a nice Italian place just down the street," David suggested. "Since I'm being thrown out of my place of work and shanghaied to dinner, I think I might be able to suggest where we can eat."

"Sounds like a plan," Carl said, heading to his office. "Now if you'll excuse me, I have a family to go home to. You kids have a good time. Don't stay out too late: we have a curfew in this town."

"He really cares about you," remarked Charlie as Carl went out the door.

"Yeah, Carl's the best friend I ever had," David said firmly. "We went through a lot together in the Gulf. Things happened over there that changed us both. I guess you need to get back to the hotel to change?"

"Yes, I do," Charlie said, picking up her purse. "I'll meet you in the lobby at around six."

David drove back to the house, thinking about how his life had changed in the past few days. He knew that he had been on a downward spiral, and that Carl had pulled him out of it with giving him this murder case. Charlie Warren's entrance into his life had made things easier, if not more interesting.

It felt strange to go out to dinner with another woman, he thought as he waited for Charlie in the lobby. I guess its part of not being married any more, he thought, looking at his watch.

The elevator opened, and Charlie came out. She dressed in a deep green dress that set off her auburn hair beautifully. Around her neck was a small Celtic gold cross. She looked enchanting. David could not believe how beautiful she looked.

Apparently his astonishment was visible. "I do clean up well on occasion, David," Charlie said, taking his arm. "Let's go to dinner."

The restaurant was a quiet little place located on a wooded street off the main thoroughfare. It was a Victorian home that someone had converted into a restaurant. Charlie and David found a quiet corner where they could spend some time together.

"I must say, David, I was a little nervous when you told me that you wanted to go to an Italian restaurant," Charlie said after their meal was over. "But this was really wonderful. The food was almost as good as it is in Italy."

"Thank you, Madam," replied David. "The owner is a retired cop whose parents came from Italy after the war. He'll be happy you approve." David looked at his glass.

"Charlie, I meant to ask you something."

"Go ahead David," Charlie said. Her face caught the candlelight in a soft, reflective way. Her green eyes danced with merriment, "ask me anything."

"Why are you here?" asked David. "Why does that letter mention you specifically?"

"Because the killer knows me, David," Charlie replied quietly. "He knows who I am, and he knows that I had to come to America once he struck. That is why I am here."

David was puzzled. "How does he know who you are? Is this someone you knew from a case somewhere? Why is he using this 'Jack the Ripper' motif? It makes no sense to me."

"It will make sense to you in time, David. I have an idea what's going on, but right now I'm going to reserve judgment on it, and see what happens. Once we know a little more about the facts of this case, I'll share my impressions about what I suspect.

I'm not trying to hold anything back from you; it's just that I want to preserve your sense of objectivity about the case."

"That's an interesting statement, Charlie." David observed. "I'm flattered that you have a good opinion of my abilities as an investigator. Believe me, over the past few months I've been wondering if my abilities to work as a detective were gone forever."

Charlie took a sip from her glass of water. She stared at the glass for a moment, weighing the words she was about to say. "I was trained as a scientist, David. I have spent most of my life in laboratories studying forensic evidence, analyzing crime scenes, and investigating some of the most horrific aspects of human behavior imaginable. I am able to do my job, and keep my sanity, because I realize that there is more to life than facts, evidence, and science."

"What are you talking about?" asked David.

"I'm talking about the things that make life worth living," said Charlie, "things like your relationship with Carl. People like Angus McKendrick and James Rosson. Concepts like honor and truth and justice and valor. Those are the things that make life bearable. I could not live in a world without those things and people, David. Such a world with things that matter is worth working for, worth fighting for. That is what my life is about: trying to fight for those things, and the only way I can do that, is to have faith that God is there to help me."

David looked at her, and realized that she not only had a beautiful face, but a beautiful soul as well, a soul like Karen's: brave, truthful, and honest. "You remind me of stories I once read, Charlie. Stories about brave knights and courage and heroism," he finally said. "I suppose that sounds pretty stupid." David looked away, embarrassed. "James wasn't lying in the airport, was he? You really are very special, aren't you?"

Now it was Charlie's turn to be embarrassed. "I'm not sure what you mean by special, but no David, he wasn't lying about my ancestry. My father's line can be traced back to the Norman Conquest. My mother's line goes back even farther; back to Arthur's Britain, perhaps." She fingered the Celtic cross around her neck. "My ancestor, Sir Charles Warren, is the one whom I am named after. He was the Head of the Metropolitan Police during the Jack the Ripper murders. My family is bound up in that story, and this letter, this murder, is the latest chapter in that story."

"I'm not sure I'm following you, Charlie," David said steadily. "But I want you to know that I am listening, and that I believe you. What can I do to help you?"

Charlie laughed merrily. "You have helped me, David, by not dismissing me as a complete lunatic. I know that you have been sent by God to help me through this time."

There was silence between them for a moment. David looked at this enchanting young woman with the strange past. He had known her for only a few days, but already he could sense the beginnings of a deep bond growing between him. Mentally, he questioned the rightness of such a bond, so soon after Karen's death. Surprisingly, he found no such objection in his heart.

"Charlie, I know I've known you for a day or so," David said haltingly, "but I'm very glad that you are here in my life right now. My life was going nowhere up until a few days ago, when Carl dragged me into his office and sent me down to that airport with that ridiculous sign." They both laughed.

"Yes, thank God for Carl," said Charlie. She smiled and winked.

"Was one of your ancestors really a pirate?" David asked playfully.

"Second officer on the *Golden Hind*," said Charlie, wrinkling her nose in reply.

"Next question?"

"What is this deep and abiding hatred you seem to have for pot pies?"

Charlie shuddered. "Nasty, awful things. Jane Rosson and I used to eat them all the time when we were students together at Oxford. They were cheap, and it was all we could afford. I developed a lifelong loathing of them since then."

"Well, that explains a lot," David noted wryly. "What's the significance of the cross around your neck? I saw you wearing it when we first met at the airport, and you're wearing it now."

Charlie dropped her eyes for a moment. "It was my mother's cross, David. The cross became mine after she died. I never take it off."

David reached across the table and took her hand in his. "I'm very sorry, Charlie, if I asked too personal a question. Please forgive me."

She smiled gently back at him. "It's all right, David. You had no way of knowing. The Celtic cross is one of the ancient symbols of Christianity. I wear it in honor of my mother, and my faith in God."

"It suits you, Charlie, like it has always been part of you," David observed. "I'm still having a hard time your interests in fencing and karate, though."

Charlie laughed, brightening the mood immediately. "Give me time, Detective. You barely know me. I'm full of surprises." The impish green light in her eyes blazed forth bewitchingly.

"Right now, nothing you could say could surprise me. You're amazing."

"All right, now it's my turn," Charlie settled back in her chair. "What's the history behind you and that charming brother of yours? What kind of family produces two people who are such polar opposites?"

"Charlie, I lied to you. Bryan is really a robot. I created him in my cellar. No, you've asked a fair question," David answered. "My mom and dad were both working people. Dad was the District Attorney here in Compton. Mom was a schoolteacher. Bryan and I went to the same high school, and the only real difference was that Bryan was a genius, and I wasn't. Grades came easy for him. I was lucky if I got the occasional "B". Bryan went on to get a full scholarship to Harvard, and from there it was Harvard Medical School, an internship and residency at Massachusetts General, and so on. I got out of high school, and the day I graduated I went with my best friend Carl down to the Army recruiting station. We both signed up that day, went through Basic, Special Forces training, and wound up in the same outfit together.

"Bryan was the one who got all the attention, and I lived I in the shadow of his spotlight. My folks died in an auto crash some years ago. Bryan got the house, and he's welcome to it, as far as I'm concerned." David took a sip of water and paused for a moment, trying to say things diplomatically to Charlie.

"Bryan has always been cold and distant," David concluded. "He was that way when we were growing up, and nothing's really changed over the years. I guess that's why Carl Davis means so much to me. He's the brother I always wanted, but never had."

"I'm sorry that Bryan's the way he is, David," Charlie said sympathetically. "We can't choose our families, and sometimes what people get isn't what they deserve. I understand that. I was blessed to grow up in a loving household. My mom and dad were wonderful, and my brother Peter was not only my brother, but also my best friend. That doesn't always happen in families, but it did in mine. I realize now that what I had isn't too common. I'm sorry about your brother. You deserved better."

David smiled. "My brother has that drafty old Victorian house, and I have a life that's been interesting. I think I got the better deal. After all, it's not every day a guy like me has dinner with someone descended from pirates and Crusaders."

"Yes, well, there you are, David," Charlie said brightly. "Bryan has his medical degrees and a drafty old Victorian barn, and you get to run around with people like me." She turned serious for a moment. "I really didn't mean to pry about your family, David. I just enjoy finding out about people, what makes them the way they are."

"It makes perfect sense, Charlie, and as for me I'll take running around with pirates any day." David looked at his watch: it was almost nine-thirty. "Good grief! Where has the time gone?"

"I think we spent most of it talking, David," Charlie said, gathering her purse and coat. "Could you introduce me to your friend who runs this restaurant?"

David took her over to Angelo, the owner of the restaurant, who was also doubling that night as the floor manager. Charlie thanked him for the meal in fluent Italian. Angelo was so impressed that he took their bill and tore it up. He took Charlie's hand in a suave gesture and kissed it gratefully. Charlie blushed furiously and thanked him again.

Before they left the restaurant, Angelo pulled David over to the side. "Where and how did you get involved with someone as classy as her?"

"I don't know, buddy. It just happened." David said.

"Well, let me tell you something: don't mess it up, okay? She's wonderful!" Angelo said in a stage whisper.

David nodded. "Don't worry; I'll try not to." He then left the restaurant with Charlie.

After he drove her back to the hotel, David asked Charlie, "I'd like to know now, before I go to bed, if I can expect a knock on my door at five-thirty and an invitation for another death run?" Charlie thought for a moment.

"Would you like that?" she asked.

"Yes I would," David replied. "The guys would be very disappointed if I didn't show up wearing my new running shoes."

"Well, in that case, we can't disappoint them, can we?" Charlie said brightly.

David drove her back to the hotel. Stopping the car at the entrance, he turned to her and said. "Thank you for the evening, it was wonderful." He kissed her hand lightly.

She put her hand up to his cheek, holding it there for a moment. "You are a kind, good man, David Stone. I'm glad you are here," she said in a low voice. "I'll see you tomorrow." She opened her door, got out, and went inside.

David sat in the car for a moment. He wanted to kiss her goodnight; why hadn't he? Something inside him told him that it was not the time to do such things. For all of her warmth and openness, there was something dark in her past that was holding her back, he sensed, something that prevented her from allowing that kind of intimacy. Charlie was one of the most unusual women David had ever encountered. She was bright and funny, and totally unpretentious. Obviously well-educated, she enjoyed being around all sorts of different people in different circumstances. David thought back to the wonderful and gracious way she had complimented Angelo on the meal at the restaurant. Charlie's ability to be kind and gracious without condescension was amazing. The term "lady" kept swimming up into David's mind whenever he thought of her.

David realized that whenever he thought of Charlie, a smile would start to play across his lips. The little detective from England had started to warm up places in his heart that he thought had gone dead forever.

He drove back to the house, feeling better than he had in months. For the first time since Karen died, David Stone looked up at the stars, and smiled.

Charlene Warren went up to her room with similar emotions. She enjoyed the evening with David, much more than she ever expected she would. In spite of her outward behavior, Charlie was a very private person. She sensed that David was as well, and that gave her some relief.

For the first time in her life, Charlie felt the apprehension of someone being hunted. The thought that someone or something was out there, stalking her as a target, was deeply disturbing to Charlie. Before she came to America, Charlie's life had been reasonably well ordered. At least it was well ordered until that black day six months ago, when she had lost both her brother and father in a single terrible day.

Charlie consciously forced herself to move away from such thoughts as she went to bed. Angus was safe, and perhaps David was someone she might be able to trust.

As she drifted off to sleep, she prayed that Angus would be safe from the thing that terrorized him the other night... .

Charlie was back in her grandfather's old house in England, walking down the long flight of stairs to the back parlor where he had his television set. The clock she passed chimed loudly the hour: two o'clock in the morning. She could see him sitting in the chair, apparently watching some sort of videotape. As Charlie turned the corner of the door, it was apparent that Grandfather had fallen asleep watching a program. A half-smile played across Charlie's face as she reached over to touch his shoulder. Her hand touched him, and the cold unyieldingness of his body stunned her. Michael Warren was not sleeping; he was dead. Charlie tore her gaze away from her dead grandfather's body to see what it was he was watching. On the screen before her was the image of her brother Peter in his last moments of life as an IRA soldier put a bullet through his head. The man who executed him turned towards the camera and laughed... .

She screamed with horror at the scene as she threw her grandfather's body onto the floor, trying to revive him with breathing and chest compressions. It was too late. The sound of the laughing man went on and on and on. Charlie stopped her ears with her hands to stop the sound, but it was no use... .

Charlie woke from the dream with a start, tears streaming down her face. She rolled over in bed and realized that she had been asleep for only a few hours. Daylight was far off, and she felt very alone. Charlie needed to talk to someone, so she dialed up David's number. The phone rang once, then twice. She was in the process of putting the phone back on the receiver when she heard his voice.

"Hello?" He did not sound sleepy.

"David, this is Charlie. I... I need to talk to you right now. I'm sorry if I woke you up, and I know it's late. Is there a chance we could meet somewhere and talk?"

"Sure Charlie," to her everlasting gratitude, David did not sound at all upset about this bizarre request. "Do you want me to meet you somewhere, or do you want to come over or want me to come over? Take your pick."

"I guess that Sophie's would be okay," Charlie finally decided.

"All right, I'll see you in about ten minutes." As she hung up, Charlie realized that for the first time in her life, she was completely vulnerable, and she had just let another person come to her aid.

Ten minutes later Charlie was over in a booth at Sophie's, telling David about her dream, and the awful events that inspired it.

David sat on the opposite seat, drinking his coffee and listening intently. He did not interrupt once, but allowed her to sort through all of the awful feelings. When it was over, Charlie broke down and wept. David silently handed her a napkin. She composed herself as she dried her tears. David reached across the table and took her hand in his.

"No one should have to carry around inside what you've been carrying all these months, Charlie," he said gently, stroking her hand. "When Karen died, my world collapsed. I tried to press on, shrug it off, like nothing had happened. I paid for my carelessness, and I nearly wrecked my whole life.

"That was in the past, though. I know a little more than I did back then. I thought I could run away from my grief, from Karen's death. That was a mistake, and I know that now. My wife is dead, and I will never see her again, never hold her in my arms again, and never make love to her again. Those are the facts of my life, and I must live with them.

"You must live with your facts, Charlie. I know I barely know you, but I also can spot someone who's been through something horrible. This talk happened sooner than I expected, but I knew that eventually we would have a conversation like this."

"You're right, David," Charlie said gratefully. "You know, you would have made a splendid psychiatrist or a minister."

"No I wouldn't, Charlie," laughed David. "I'd probably shoot or strangle some of the whiny nut cases before I'd analyze them. I'm much too intolerant and impatient to do something like that."

"Liar," Charlie laughing in return. "You just passed your first clinical practicum with flying colors."

"Well, thank you, Doctor," David yawned prodigiously. "Excuse me, but it's getting late, and if I remember correctly, you were going to send my middle-aged body on another death run tomorrow."

"Yes, I did promise you that, didn't I?" remembered Charlie. They paid their bill and walked outside into the cool summer night. David walked her over to her car.

"Good night," he said. Reaching down, he kissed her lightly on her cheek. Charlie kissed him in return, and they held each other for a moment.

"Thank you for listening, David." she said gratefully. "I'll see you tomorrow." She got into her car and drove off.

She'll probably be at my door tomorrow, he thought, telling me that she was frightened and vulnerable and that the kiss was a mistake and so on. That's the way it usually worked, wasn't it? He shook his head to clear it, and headed home for a few hours of sleep.

4

The phone rang promptly at five. It was Charlie, letting David know brightly that she was on her way. Predictably, his body felt as though someone had beaten him with a tire iron. David managed to pull on his jogging suit just in time to answer the knock on the door.

He tottered over to the door and let Charlie in. "You're just in time to see me put on my new running shoes the troops gave me."

She wrinkled her nose at the color. "Goodness, they are vile, aren't they? But they are good shoes. Your feet should feel better."

"That's a start. At least two parts of my body will feel okay. All I have to do is not look at the color, then I won't throw up," grumped David. "Before we start, could you beat my body with a baseball bat so I can feel better while we run?"

"Don't be a baby, David," Charlie coaxed, giving him a smile which strangely made him feel much better. "You'll stretch out in a little bit."

Their run to the hotel was at roughly the same pace as it was the day before. David managed to keep up with Charlie (or rather she let him keep up with her). He was not breathing as heavily as he was on the previous day, which gave him some sort of hope that things would get better. David was smart enough to realize that Charlie had sized up his physical abilities and was not going to allow him to get hurt. It was easier today for him because Charlie made it that way.

Charlie wasn't even winded. "You're doing better today," she observed brightly.

"Thanks coach, but I know you're lying," he puffed. "Is this going to be the daily routine from now on?"

Charlie thought for a moment. "I'm enjoying running with you. Are you getting something out of it?" she finally asked.

"Yes, Charlie, I am," David replied, looking directly at Charlie. "I like a lot of the things that have happened in the last few days." She dropped her eyes. "I want you to know that I was happy to listen to you last night."

"Thank you, David. That means a lot to me. You were very understanding." Her tone changed. "Are you up for some more grease and cholesterol at Sophie's?"

"Why not?" he replied. They went over to the diner, which was populated with the usual early morning crowd. All of the cops and regulars were eagerly anticipating their arrival. David's new shoes drew a chorus of whistles and shouts of approval. There were two cups of coffee waiting for them at a booth, and the cook informed them that their omelets were being cooked.

"This is the problem with a small town," David told Charlie. "There are no secrets here, and news travels like lightning. I expect that Angelo called up Carl last night and told him about you."

"Really? Do you think so?" Charlie was genuinely surprised. "All I did was thank him for the meal."

"No, you thanked him in Italian, Charlie," David corrected. "You complemented him in his native language. That honored him, and it honored his restaurant. It was a beautiful thing. People like things like that. It shows class and character. The world needs more of that, and they need more people like you around."

Charlie blushed. She's so beautiful, David thought. I couldn't possibly have the luck to get involved with someone like her, someone like Karen... .

The arrival of the omelets interrupted his reverie. "Are you back on the ground, David?" Charlie asked politely. "I was just asking you what you've got planned for today?"

"Of course, I'm sorry. David stumbled around for a second. He was beginning to notice that when Charlie was around he had a hard time concentrating. "I was thinking of organizing an area with all of our data out where we could see it." David responded. "We could use the briefing room. It has enough space, and I'm sure Carl won't mind. I'd like you to talk to Joan about her crime scene report. I've skimmed it, and it looks very detailed. There might be some areas and questions you might have or some angles she may have missed. I know Joan very well, and I'm sure she won't mind.

"We need to go to the crime scene itself and have Angus with us. I know it may be rough on him, but it's his church, and he's the only one who might know if something's not quite right. That's for starters; can you think of anything else?"

Charlie thought for a moment. "No, I think you have it well covered. I think we may have a problem with your brother, though. My observations wounded his pride, and people like that generally throw up roadblocks and other sorts of passive-aggressive acts when their vanity is pricked."

"Do you really think so?" David ladled on the sarcasm. "Are you sure you've never met Bryan before, because that's exactly the way he is."

Charlie smiled. "I've had more than my share of prima donnas and blowhards. Bryan's just another member of a very large species of bureaucrats with over inflated egos."

"Well, Compton might be minus a specimen, if my brother doesn't watch himself. If he gives you a hard time, I will personally rearrange several of his body parts." David threatened ominously. Charlie laughed merrily at his comments. I love hearing her laugh, David thought to himself.

"So what do you need to do today, Charlie?" he asked. "I would like your assistance in all of this, but I realize you have other duties and engagements as well."

"No, I think today my time is yours," Charlie said brightly.

"Well, drive me home and let's get started," David said, paying for their food. Charlie drove him home, where he showered and changed quickly. This time he raced to the station ahead of her, trying to preempt any sort of practical jokes his station colleagues might have arranged in anticipation of his and Charlie's arrival.

Carl motioned him into his office. David went in and Carl closed the door.

"I've already told all of the division chiefs to make sure their people lay off of you and Charlie," he said. "This is not a dating game show we're running here. It's a police force, and I just want you to know that before anything else is said and done."

"I understand that, Carl, and I appreciate it as well." David responded gratefully. "

"I would like to add on a personal note, that I like the improvement I've seen in your attitude in the last few days. It wouldn't have anything to do with the arrival of a little red-haired detective from England, would it?"

"It might."

"That's what I thought." Carl grunted, shaking his head. "Buddy, you have no idea what you've got yourself into. Let me tell you why: Charlie Warren had guys crawling all over her at the Academy. She brushed them all off; didn't have time for any of them. I saw it happen, so I know what I'm talking about. She's normally very friendly with everyone, but with you, it's different. That's why I'm saying that you've got something going with her that's pretty special."

David looked at Carl strangely. "Carl, she's from England. She's a noted authority in forensics. Do you think she'd give all of that up to come over here to this sleepy little town and take up with someone like me? I'm just some dumb cop from the sticks."

"That's nonsense, Dave," Carl said, looking him straight in the eye. "I saw the reports on you in the Army. You could have gone into CIA, NSA, and anything else for that matter. They practically begged you to come on board. You turned them down flat. You came back to Compton. You chose to be here. Why couldn't she make the same choice?"

"Why would she make that choice, Carl?" David replied. "I have family here; she doesn't."

"Yes she does, Dave," Carl said. "Angus McKendrick is her godfather. Charlie has no living relatives in England. Her parents are both dead. Her brother Peter was in the SAS and was killed by IRA extremists. They mailed her grandfather a videotape of his torture and execution at their hands. He had a heart attack and died the same day he got the tape. Charlie found him. That happened six months ago."

"She told me that last night, Carl," David said quietly. "I couldn't believe it. What a rotten break in life she's had. She called me up last night after she'd had a bad dream about it. We went over to Sophie's and she told me."

"Well, I'm glad she did," Carl said approvingly. "Look, Dave, I'm not going to tell you how to run your life, but Charlie Warren's a really special girl. Maybe this is God's way of working things out so that both of you can find a little happiness. Who knows? Just enjoy being around her, and see how things go, okay?"

Carl shifted gears. "Do you want to use the briefing room to set up your stuff on the Thatcher case?"

"Yes I do, Carl. Charlie thinks that Bryan is going to cause trouble on the Examiner end."

Charlie came into the office with a smile for both of them. "I want you to notice, Dave, that when the word 'trouble' is mentioned, Charlie Warren appears. This is not an accident," Carl grinned. Charlie gave a little curtsey in reply. "What's on your list of things to do, Doctor?"

"I'll handle Bryan, since I'm the one who stepped on his sand castle," she volunteered brightly.

"Well, just watch your step, kiddo," cautioned Carl. "Bryan has a reputation for playing rough when he's crossed."

"Fiddlesticks!" retorted Charlie, coloring a bit. "I eat types like Bryan Stone for lunch."

Carl threw up his hands in mock surrender. "I believe you. I saw what happened at the Academy, Charlie. Believe me, people still talk about what happened."

"I can start working on that wall," David said firmly, "while Charlie reads the crime scene report."

"Well, enjoy yourselves, you two, because I have to take care of all of those media people who are starting to call me every five minutes." Carl massaged his head. "I already have a splitting headache."

David went to work posting all of the evidence and reports on the briefing room board, leaving plenty of space for more data as it came in. Carl started fielding calls from the newspapers and media outlets. Thanks to the murderer's letter and package to the *Post,* people were beginning to take note of the murder investigation going on in Compton. It would make things difficult for the investigation team, having reporters and journalists crawling all over things. The Mayor's office was starting to get into the act as well, along with other bureaucratic types. Carl's plate, already full, was starting to spill over.

Charlie was the one who saved him. She came into his office after a few hours and proposed that she handle the PR front with the press. It was only fair, she told him. Carl was grateful for the offer of help, but he wasn't sure if the British government would approve.

"Leave that to me," she said, dialing up James Rosson at the Consulate. "James? Yes, it's me. No, things are going along all right here. No, I haven't started a new war. Yes, the Americans are still on our side. Will you please stop teasing me for a moment? Listen, Carl Davis is about ready to have a stroke dealing with the press. I've asked if I could step in and help him. Do you have any official objections to that? What? Of course I can be diplomatic! Why are you laughing, James? No, I don't think we'll wind up having to fight the Americans again in addition to everyone else."

She stamped her foot. "Keep on laughing James, I don't care, because if you don't stop, James Rosson, I'll tell Jane about you, and then you'll be in big trouble. All right, that's better. Yes, we're looking forward to seeing all of you on Saturday. Love to Jane! Bye."

She hung up the phone. "I'm now the official Press Liaison Officer for the Compton Police Department." she said.

"Trouble at the Consulate?" Carl beatifically asked. "Anything you want to share with us, Doctor?"

"No Carl, and stop that," Charlie said, sticking her tongue out at him. "You know Sarah and I are good friends, so watch yourself."

"Yes, madam." Carl mockingly bowed. She wrinkled her nose in reply.

Charlie immediately went to work. While David was setting up their work in the briefing room, Charlie was busy contacting all of the news services in the New York area. After composing a brief statement to the press, she sent it to all of the news services, listing herself as the contact officer for the Compton city police department. Carl was amazed how swiftly she handled all of the perplexing and ridiculous questions in such short order.

"If I weren't married, I'd marry you, Charlie," Carl said as he watched her put to rest all of the media headaches that had been driving him crazy for the past few days.

As David worked in the briefing room, he started to realize just how much of a personal threat Charlie was working under. The letter to the *Post* was more than a mocking challenge; it was a direct threat to Charlie's personal safety. The thought of someone wanting to hurt someone as brave and courageous as Charlie Warren enraged him.

"I'm going to make it my job in life to get you before you get her," he grated under his breath as he pinned the letter to the board. His anger stopped him from realizing that Charlie had quietly come up beside him. She put a hand on his shoulder, which caused him to nearly topple off of the small stool he was standing on.

"You can't let your personal feelings cloud your judgment, David," Charlie said, "though I appreciate the concern."

David turned around. "Charlie, did you bring a weapon with you to America?"

She smiled. "Of course I did, David. Here it is." She opened the jacket she was wearing over her blouse to reveal a holstered Glock. "Do you feel better?"

"I'd feel better if I could see how well you handle that thing," David replied with some heat. "Maybe I'm just a little overprotective, okay?"

"Uh oh, here it comes," chimed in Carl, who had just walked into the briefing room. "You're in for it now, buddy."

Charlie shot a warning glance in Carl's direction. Taking the comment in stride, She said to David: "I understand your concerns. Would you feel better if I show you that I can handle a pistol?"

"Yes, I would." David replied.

They went down to the basement firing range. It was small by any police department's standards but it was adequate for the Compton Police Department. Carl pinned a target onto a frame and sent it down the range lane.

"Any time you're ready, Charlie." Carl said with a strange look on his face. He knew what was coming; David did not.

Charlie adjusted the ear protection muffs over her ears. She turned to Carl and nodded. It was over in about five seconds of unbelievable noise and smoke. In that time, Charlie had drawn her weapon, sighted down the target, and put ten jacketed slugs into a space no wider than a dime. The target had barely moved five feet.

"Didn't I tell you, Dave, that Charlie not only taught forensic analysis at the FBI Academy, but was the assistant head of weapons training?" Carl asked after his ears stopped ringing.

David surrendered gallantly. "No, you failed to mention that little fact. Okay, guys, I'm a believer. I guess I owe you lunch."

"You owe me a lot more than that, cowboy," Charlie playfully said, punching his shoulder lightly.

"I have complete confidence that you can handle a weapon, and NO, I am not stupid enough to ask for a personal demonstration of your ability to defend yourself in hand-to-hand combat." David said, trying to clear his ears.

"Wise move, grasshopper," noted Carl. "Can we get back to work, children?"

Charlie read the crime scene report from front to back. She agreed with David that it was very good, but she also wanted to go down to the church again to get a feel for the situation. She put a call into Bryan's office. Bryan, of course, was unavailable, but a message was left and he would return the call when he had the time.

"Which means 'never'", translated Charlie. "We'll give him until the end of the day, and then I'll start rattling some bigger cages down the line."

"That will not be pretty," observed David. "Bryan detests administrative end runs around him, except when he's the one who causes them and they work to his advantage."

"Then he needs to learn to play fair and share his toys. Kindergarten 101," Charlie said blithely. "Shall we go see Uncle Angus?"

"What an excellent idea, old girl," said David, in his best (at least in his mind) British accent. "Shall we be off?" This earned him another punch on the shoulder from Charlie.

"Just for that, I'm driving," she said. "Shut up and get in the car."

"Did you hear that, Carl?" David turned to Carl in mock horror, "this nice little English girl told me to shut up. How rude!"

"You're lucky that's all she didn't do to you, Ace," advised Carl. "Get out of my station before I tell her to do something really bad to you."

They left the station and drove down to Trinity. Angus was in the rectory studying his Bible in preparation for Sunday morning service. He had the ability, honed through many years of practice, to selectively ignore distractions. After several minutes of rapidly escalating knocks, he finally answered the door.

"If you'd waited a few more minutes, I was going to have Charlie kick the door down," David said. "I would have used a battering ram, but she's capable of opening doors with a simple pivot kick. That's why I take her along. She's useful that way."

"I would have used your head as a battering ram before I would have bothered doing that." quipped Charlie, embracing Angus and kissing him.

Angus was delighted to see them. "Charlie! David! What a wonderful surprise! I was just planning to ring you up to see if you could come over and have lunch with me." Shaking David's hand, he saw his face. "But I see that this is not a social call, is it?"

Charlie hugged Angus again. "Business can wait until after lunch, can't it, David?"

David was happy for a break. "Of course we can wait. Angus, we just wanted to look around the church again, if it's not too much trouble."

Charlie took Angus' arm. "Is there anything I can do to help you get things ready?"

"Do you know what a kitchen is?" asked David incredulously. This earned him a venomous look.

Angus came to his rescue. "No, love, there isn't. But you can help me on Sunday, though. Would you do a reading from the Old Testament at Sunday morning's service?"

"Of course I will, Uncle Angus," Charlie said. "I'm deeply honored. I'll make sure David is along as well." She turned her head towards him and stuck out her tongue. "He needs to be in church, after the things he's said to me today."

"It's true, Father McKendrick. I have sinned grievously." David said in mock contrition. "I questioned the lady's ability to use a firearm. I also made fun of her lovely English accent, and accused her of wanting to batter down your door with a pivot kick. Worst of all, I implied that she didn't know what a kitchen was."

Angus laughed. "Those are certainly serious transgressions, my son. I'll leave your punishment up to God," he winked at Charlie. "I'm sure justice will prevail. Though a word of warning to you might be in order: Charlie's father, brother, and godfather were all in British Intelligence, so she's been very well trained, you might say."

Angus had already prepared lunch, in anticipation of a positive response from his offer. David observed this and made a comment to that effect. "I know my goddaughter, and her powers of persuasion," he said, bringing out the trays. "The acceptance of the invitation to lunch was a foregone conclusion."

It was a wonderful lunch. Charlie and Angus talked nonstop about England, Scotland, and just about everything else in the world except the murder. David sat back and just enjoyed the experience of watching two people who shared a deep bond with each other. Two hours passed before anyone was aware of it.

David finally looked at this watch. "I hate to break this up, but we really do need to go through the church sometime today."

"David's right, Charlie," Angus said, standing up and taking the trays away. "I've been very selfish with your time. You have work to do."

"Nonsense," David said. "It's been delightful. I've enjoyed just sitting back, watching you two and listening to you talk. I could have spent the whole day with you both."

"Thank you, David." responded Angus. "We will have to continue this sometime soon. Let me take you over to the church." He ushered them down a narrow side corridor to a dark oaken door which opened into the church sanctuary.

"This door was locked Sunday night?" David asked.

"Yes, I locked it myself," Angus replied. "We're too small a church to afford night security people and all that. I personally checked all the doors and entrances before retiring that night."

The church was deeply quiet as they entered. The red light flickered over the sanctuary, and the only other sources of light came from the brilliantly lit stained glass windows and the light on the cross over the altar. The reflected glow from its oaken surface cast a serene light on the interior of the church. The sanctuary was filled with a deep sense of peace.

Charlie picked up on this immediately. "Evil has tried to assail this place, but it has failed," she said in hushed tones. She walked slowly to where the altar was.

Angus nodded. "I have been in many great cathedrals in my life: Canterbury, York, Westminster, Notre' Dame, but in all of those places I have never felt the sense of holiness and peace that I feel when I am in this sanctuary."

"That is because this is your home, Angus. You belong here," observed Charlie. "Maybe this could be my home too," she added in a tone so low that no one caught it.

The overwhelming grief from the murder on Sunday caught up with Angus in a sudden rush. "That poor girl," he brokenly cried, collapsing to his knees in front of the altar.

Charlie rushed to his side, kneeling down next to him. "Angus, dear Angus, she is at peace now. She found her way home to God. Christ has claimed her soul. Know that and be at peace. That is why this church was desecrated. The devil lost a soul, so he had to do something hideously spiteful out of frustrated anger." She held onto him, holding him close. "You are a good servant of God. You are not responsible for her death."

David stood back in silence, watching Charlie comfort Angus. There seemed to be a holy light overshadowing them both. The silence and peace filled the air with a stillness as they shared their grief with God. David knew he was in the presence of something holy. It was something he had never seen before, or felt in his whole life.

At last, the moment was over, and life rushed back in on them all. Charlie rose up from Angus and pointed towards the rear door.

"He came through there, after forcing open the rear door. Jenny was dragged over to the altar. Her body was taken from the bag, raised up and nailed to the cross."

She stooped down to the carpet next to the altar. "I see some small gray fibers which are a different color from the red of the carpet. Joan must have missed them. She produced a small patch of tape and an evidence bag from her purse. "We'll take these back to the station for processing"

David went over to Angus, who was now sitting on the front pew. "I don't know why I didn't ask you before now, but do you remember the name of the cab company you called to pick Jenny up? Did you see the cab?"

Angus answered promptly. "It was a cab from the Green Cab Company, and its number was 506."

David suddenly remembered something. "There was a cab stolen from the Green Cab Company Sunday night. It hasn't been found yet."

Charlie reached for her cell phone. Dialing it, she spoke to Carl. "Carl, this is Charlie, has anyone found that Green cab that was reported stolen yet? No? Well, it was probably used by the killer to pick up Jenny Thatcher. Yeah, I hope we find it too. Bye."

She turned to David. "The killer most likely used the cab to pick up Jenny. Since it was stolen, and he knew the police would be looking for it, he wouldn't use it for any great length of time. He would probably drive the cab to a predetermined location where he could transfer Jenny to his car, then take her to where he operated on her."

"That cab is somewhere close, within a few miles of this place, probably off on a side road." Charlie said quickly. "He wouldn't have a lot of time to dispose of it, so there's a good chance it will be intact."

"The train station is only half a mile away," David said. Once Jenny found out that she wasn't being taken to the train station, she'd try to escape. He'd have to find a spot to overpower her and get her out of sight quickly. A screaming girl in the back of a car attracts attention."

Charlie walked over to Angus. "Thank you again, Uncle Angus, for everything."

He rose up from the pew, and they embraced. "I give you my solemn word, before God, before Christ my savior, we will track down and bring the man who did this to justice." she vowed.

"I know you will, Charlie. May Almighty God protect you both." Angus said in a farewell blessing to them as they left the church.

They said nothing for a few moments after they got into the car. David was pondering all of the things he had heard and seen in the sanctuary. There was a quiet power about Charlie that had suddenly become very apparent to him. He had seen it revealed in the sanctuary, in the way she had taken command of the situation, and in the way she had comforted Angus McKendrick. She possessed a nobility and strength in her that came from a source that was not of this world.

David's cell phone rang as they were driving back to the police station. It was Carl. "Good job, guys, they found the cab two miles west of town on a side road. Joan's headed there now."

"We are too, Carl. Thanks," David hung up. "We need to follow Main two miles out west. They found the cab on a side road." David told Charlie. "I'll show you where Bryan lives on our way out of town. It's right before where we're going" He gave her directions as they headed out of town.

They met Joan Richards and her crime scene team at the site. The cab was about half a mile off of the main road leading east out of town. It was a fairly deserted stretch of road, and the nearest house was about two miles away.

Joan was already out, taking photographs. "It looks like it's in good shape," she said, winding her camera. "He didn't have time to torch it."

"He wouldn't want to do that anyway," Charlie said. "A burning car draws attention, and that's something he didn't want to do right then. Do you see any footprints around the car? By the way, I'm Charlie Warren. David seems to be forgetting his manners this afternoon." Charlie held out her hand and Joan shook it.

"Yeah, well David's rather distracted at the moment," Joan said knowingly. The two women immediately understood each other. Charlie smiled slightly and Joan winked at her prodigiously.

"What are you two talking about?" David asked.

"Completely clueless, what did I tell you? David's a bright boy in most things, but some things are a little hard for him to grasp." Joan shook her head mightily. "See if there are any tire tracks on the ground, Dave, while I go get some plaster cooking. You can come and help me, Charlie."

"I'm not that stupid, Joan. What's going on in that evil brain of yours?" David asked suspiciously. Joan Richards had a maternal streak a mile wide, which David had found amusing, until now. Charlie's eyes flickered with amusement as she watched David's bewilderment.

"Mind your own business, cowboy. Charlie, let's go make some mud," Joan replied. The two women went back to Joan's van, leaving a puzzled David to examine the tire tracks on the ground. He looked closely. It had rained that Saturday prior to the murder, so the ground had been soft that night. "I think I see some. In fact, it looks like about my size." He pointed to two faint shoe impressions over by the driver's side of the cab.

Coming back to the area where David was, Charlie noticed that the footprints stopped at the rear passenger door, where it was obvious that another, smaller pair of feet had landed on the ground, and they seemed to be apart. "The ground here is disturbed, as though two people were struggling." She stepped gingerly around and looked away from the cab. "There seem to be some footprints leading away from the cab, again, two different sets." Charlie walked off from the cab for about ten feet, stopping at an area where the foliage seemed disturbed. "Jenny ran away from him. He caught her, knocked her down, and then tied her up."

Joan followed her over to the area, snapping pictures and taking care not to disturb the trail. "Good work, Charlie. I can see a second set of tire tread marks by the cab. Let me take pictures of those and set some casting material on them so we can pick up some impressions."

"The male shoes lead over to those tread marks," Charlie noted. "At that point, he was probably carrying her."

Joan busily worked on the tire tracks while David and Charlie dusted the car for fingerprints. The door handles had been wiped clean, but the inside might prove to be another story.

The detectives all worked as a team in a slow, methodical fashion. No one hurried; everyone took their time to do things right. The practiced manner in which Charlie fell into the routine gave David a great deal of confidence.

Once the exterior exam of the cab was completed, the trunk was opened. "I don't see any gross sign of blood, but you never know," Charlie said. She produced her evidence bag from her purse. "Joan, I picked up some gray fibers from the church carpet this afternoon. Maybe they match the interior of the cab."

"Possibly," Joan noted. "Or they could match our mystery van. Those tracks are definitely some sort of minivan."

"Of course," Charlie said, "a minivan would give him enough space to immobilize her further for transport to his laboratory. He might even have had a small mechanical ventilator on board in case he decided to paralyze her."

"Or he may have simply tied her up and covered her with a blanket," David said, peering through the glass. "I see no signs of a struggle in here, but I'll reserve final judgment on that until Joan and her weird science guys give this cab a thorough inspection."

"Do you think this guy has some sort of secret lab out in this direction, Charlie?" asked Joan, "I mean, it's wide open, and there are not many people living around here."

"Possible but unlikely," Charlie said, "Rural people may live far apart, but they're connected in other ways. A stranger out here would attract attention. In fact, a farmer is the one who called in the report about the cab this afternoon."

"Well, I've got to call for a tow truck to come out and get this clunker to the impound lot so my boys and I can give it a thorough inspection. Thanks for coming out this afternoon. It was a real pleasure watching you work, Charlie."

Charlie blushed slightly. "Thank you, Joan. I appreciate the compliment."

"See you guys around campus," Joan said, winking broadly at David, who scowled in reply.

On their way back into town, David asked Charlie how she got into forensic work.

"I grew up on a diet of detective stories, movies, and television shows. My father got me interested in karate. I've been doing that since I was ten."

"That explains your prowess in martial arts," observed David. "Angus said your dad was in British Intelligence, is that right?"

Charlie suddenly became very quiet. "Yes David, that's right. He disappeared twelve years ago while over in Europe. We haven't heard from him since. Two years ago, Grandfather got a call from MI6, saying that they believed that he was dead, but they were not sure."

"I'm very sorry, Charlie," David said sincerely. "I didn't want to pry into your life, or hurt you in any way."

"I know that, David," Charlie said softly, "I know you didn't mean to hurt me. In fact, you are one of the most considerate people I've ever met. It's refreshing to meet a man with your gentleness, tact, and discretion. Your parents did a beautiful job in raising you."

"And then there's Bryan." added David, trying to cheer her up.

It worked. Charlie laughed. "Yes, the great family riddle. You know, are you sure he's related to you? Talk about polar opposites."

"Yes, unfortunately, he is related to me. My non-identical twin." They pulled into the station parking lot.

Carl was waiting for them. "Looks like you two have had a good day," he observed. "Bryan's office has reluctantly sent over his report on Jenny Thatcher." He held up an impressively bound document.

Charlie took it from him. "Oh goody, I can hardly wait."

"Be nice," David warned.

Charlie went into the briefing room and sat down in a chair. It took her the rest of the afternoon to read the Medical Examiner's report. About halfway through the ordeal she asked David for a pen and a legal pad. By the time she was done, she had covered both sides of two pages of the pad with neat, precise notes.

David busied himself with reviewing witness reports from the EMTs and the nurses at the ER who worked on Jenny when she arrived at the ER. A snort from Charlie signified that she was finished; also that she had reached her limits of patience.

"A first year medical student could have done a better job than this." she tossed the offending document down on the table with a contemptuous flourish.

"Do tell," said David, folding his hands and looking at Charlie with an owlish expression. "Do you mean to say that my brilliant brother's efforts have failed to impress you?"

Charlie transfixed him with a withering glance. "Yes," she said. The single word carried all the contempt she could muster.

"Does this mean we are going back to the Medical Examiner's office for another session with 'ET'?" asked David innocently.

"No it does not," retorted Charlie in a sharp tone. "It means that I am going over there by myself and dismantle that pompous twit. His report is so full of holes that it borders on gross incompetence."

David had not seen this side of Charlie's personality before. Few people had, and those that did, never forgot it once they had been exposed to it. Charlie could not tolerate laziness or incompetence. Bryan's treatment of her at the office was one thing, but to deliberately and indifferently turn out shoddy piece of medical forensics was outrageous.

Carl entered the briefing room. He immediately sensed the danger signs. "Okay, guys, what's wrong?" He turned to David. "What did you do to her now?"

"He did nothing wrong, Carl," Charlie said grimly. "David's been perfect. It's that misbegotten changeling brother of his that's the problem."

"Well, I hate to tell you this, but it's now time for both of you to leave this office, because unless you're on night watch, you need to be out of here." Carl paused for a moment. "Speaking of night watch, I believe you have the honors on Sunday, old buddy."

David grimaced. "Wonderful, Carl. You know how much I love that."

"Yeah, well life's hard. Now get out of here."

Charlie and David left the building together. David took a breath and decided to ask: "Charlie, what are you doing for the rest of the night?"

Charlie looked at him. "Nothing, really. I was thinking of popping over to see Uncle Angus for a bit."

"Would you mind if I tagged along?" asked David sheepishly. "I mean, if it's intruding, don't worry, just let me know."

Charlie looked at him for a moment. She had toyed earlier with the idea of asking him to come with her back to Trinity, but was afraid he might be getting tired of being around her so much. Charlie's brains and manner intimidated most men. David seemed to enjoy being around her.

"I'd love it if you came with me, David," Charlie said softly. "I was somewhat concerned that you might be getting tired of lugging me around town all the time."

"You must be joking, Charlie," David said in an astonished tone. "You're absolutely amazing to be around. Father McKendrick is a gold mine. You have quite a family; you've been everywhere, and done everything. I enjoyed listening to you two talk this afternoon. It was the best time I've had in months."

Charlie blushed, "I'm happy we've made an impression on you. But don't you think we need to get out of everyone's way and let them go home at least?" She was referring to the fact that they had halted in front of the station door while they talked, blocking the exit for all the people trying to leave the building.

"You two clowns need to decide where you're going before I arrest you for blocking a fire exit." Carl said as he brushed past them out into the parking lot. He smirked as he walked out to his car, shaking his head. David, old buddy, you're toast, Carl thought.

David drove Charlie back to Trinity, stopping at a local grocery store for supplies. Charlie called Angus and told him that she was coming over with David to cook dinner.

Angus was overjoyed at seeing them again, and he quickly fired off a list of items they needed for supper.

"And now, sir," Charlie warned as they exited the car in front of the rectory. "You will be forced to eat your words concerning my lack of experience in the kitchen."

Charlie allowed Angus and David to take the groceries into the kitchen, then promptly shooed them out. "Remember, I have a gun," she threatened.

Angus and David sat in the parlor while Charlie worked on dinner. David had the time of his life. Angus was an absolute treasure-trove of experiences, places and people. David's own father had been a taciturn, colorless individual who seemed to have little time for his family. Meeting someone like Angus was a completely unique experience for him.

Angus, on the other hand, was delighted to see his Charlie take up with such a fine, intelligent young man. He could already see the developing bond between them, and was very pleased about it. Angus had enough sense not to say anything about it to Charlie, much less David, but he was pleased, nonetheless.

"So you were trapped at Tobruk, and the Germans were closing in on your position. Did you think about surrendering?" David asked, enthralled with Angus' story.

"No, of course not, lad. The SAS never surrenders. We hunkered down, trying not to get ourselves shot to pieces, and just let the Germans have it. Eventually we broke through and made it back to our lines. We lost a lot of good men out in that desert, though." His eyes turned misty at the thought.

"Did you meet Charlie's grandfather in Libya?" David was enthralled with Angus' war experiences.

"No," replied Angus. "Michael Warren was part of the planning and intelligence section for the Special Operations Executive. That was a department set up by Churchill himself for running secret operations deep behind enemy lines. I had met Michael at Oxford a while back, and my name came up for an operation and he remembered me. So he yanked me out of Libya and sent me to some insane training camp with him and five other unfortunates for one of Winnie's special assignments. The Regular Army chaps weren't too keen on SOE. Michael Warren had a pirate streak in him, and that sort of cloak and dagger mentality appealed to him. He got along famously with Churchill, who was just like that."

"I have a feeling that Charlie may have inherited some of that as well."

"Laddie, you have no idea," Angus warned him knowingly. Charlie made an appearance at the door at the mention of her name.

"I wish you wouldn't do that," complained David.

"Do what?" Charlie was the picture of innocence.

"Show up whenever your name is mentioned. It's creepy."

"Get used to it, chum. By the way, dinner is served."

Charlie was better than her word. Angus and Charlie kept David laughing longer and harder than he had in months. After the meal was over, he insisted on doing the dishes. "I have to do something to atone for my unkind remarks," he said as he shooed them out of the kitchen.

"Doing the dishes is just the start, David. You have a lot to atone for, remember." Charlie advised him, winking at Angus. They sat in the parlor as David worked in the kitchen.

"He fits right in, doesn't he?" observed Angus, which translated into "I like him very much, and I know you do as well."

"Indeed," Charlie replied, which meant, "I like him a lot and he likes me."

"What's going on out here? I throw you two out into the parlor and I don't hear a peep from either of you. That's very ominous. When Charlie is quiet, I know that trouble is brewing," David called from the kitchen.

"Your David learns quickly, Charlie," observed Angus, smiling broadly.

"Oh, we're just taking a breather of sorts," Charlie said, wrinkling her nose at Angus, who winked prodigiously in return.

David came out to join them in the parlor. "I want you to know, sir," he said to Angus, "that Charlie and you have collectively destroyed every single stereotype I ever had concerning people from the UK."

"Well, chalk one up for the Empire," Angus said, beaming mightily. His mantle clock struck eleven.

"Is there something wrong with your clock, Uncle Angus? I just heard it strike eleven." Charlie asked.

"No, my dear, my clock is working just fine. It's your clock, and David's that's off." Angus replied.

"Well, it's way past everyone's bedtime, so we all need to say good night, I think." David said, standing up and stretching. "Your goddaughter has been forcing me to accompany her on five mile runs in the morning."

"An interesting development," observed Angus, finally succumbing to the urge to tease his goddaughter. "Charlie usually never runs with anyone. You used to tell me, Charlie that you hated running with other people, didn't you?" Angus' remarks earned him a dirty look from Charlie, who then winked at him and smiled and gave him a big hug.

Angus ushered them out the door and into the cool night. "I'll see you both on Sunday, if not before," he said, waving to them as they got into David's car.

My Charlie is in love, he thought with wonder as he watched the car drive off. Perhaps the Lord would be gracious to him and allow him to see her finally happy. He smiled and went back into the rectory.

David drove Charlie back to the hotel. On the way, he told her how wonderful it had been to be with them both, and he thanked Charlie for allowing him to be part of her evening. He went around and opened her door.

Charlie got out of the door and said to David, "If you don't kiss me here and now, I don't know what I'll do." She threw her arms around David and he kissed her, holding her like he'd never let her go.

For David, it felt like a dream. "Charlie," he breathed into her ear, "I've wanted to kiss you ever since I saw you at that airport." He kissed her again, stroking her hair.

"I started falling for you ever since I saw you with that ridiculous sign," she replied teasingly. They held each other close for a moment.

"Well, I really need to go inside and get some rest," she said reluctantly. "I'll see you tomorrow."

"Are we going on our little run?" David asked.

"No, I have to be up early tomorrow to get ready for my encounter with your brother." Charlie said. "Besides, you need a bit of a breather from that anyway. We'll do it on Saturday."

"I'll see you tomorrow, then." David said as she walked to the hotel entrance. "I love you," he called to her as she opened the door. Charlie turned around and smiled at him from the door.

"I have wonderful hearing, David," she called from the door, closing it with a big smile. David in turn got back into his car, and somehow managed to drive back home without killing himself or anyone else. He went to bed convinced he had spent the better part of the evening living some sort of dream.

Charlie went to bed serenely happy for the first time in months. So much for not being ready, she thought, dismissing that notion from her mind forever.

In Charlie's short stay in Compton, she had grown to love the small town and its people. England, for all of its charm and history, had held little joy for her. The post at Bramshill was dry and unexciting, and she had tired of the endless grind of academic life. The afternoon Charlie had spent with Joan Richards and David had been exhilarating for her, from professional and personal standpoints. She thought of Trinity and how much it reminded her of the small English church from her childhood. Charlie missed home and family. England had held little of that for her after that black day six months ago.

Angus was the only family that she had left, and she noted how well he had settled into life in America. She was confident that God had led her to this place, and that she could make that transition as well. As she drifted off to sleep, Charlie realized that she had not thought about the murder of Jenny Thatcher for at least several hours.

She woke up, sitting upright in bed, paralyzed with terror. In the corner by the window stood a figure. It was shrouded in black. She blinked her eyes to clear her mind, to purge the image from her sight. It was still there; it was real. The room was deadly cold, thick with the cloying odor of death and decay.

Who are you? Her mind screamed at the phantasm.

Death, I am Death, came the silent words to her brain.

Consciously, she forced herself to speak words out loud to the intruder. "You will leave me, now. In the name of God, GO!"

With those words that she somehow croaked out, the thing collapsed into nothingness, and the warmth of the late summer night flowed back into the room. Charlie fell back onto the bed, and remembered nothing more … .

5

Charlie woke that morning to the sound of her telephone ringing. It was David:

"Now it's my turn to wake you up, sleepyhead."

"Good morning," she replied sleepily. "Was I dreaming about last night, or did it happen?"

"Not unless dreams are infectious, because we both experienced it. Come to think of it, maybe dreams are infectious. If that's the case, then I never want to be cured."

Lying back on the pillow, Charlie played with the sheet. "Neither do I. What are you going to be doing today?"

David paused for a moment. "I have to go into New York to pick up some more information from the Medical Examiner's office. After I come back, Joan and I are then going to go over her crime scene analysis. That's my plan for today. You're going to the ME's office here in town, right?"

"That's the plan," Charlie said, stretching luxuriously, "I need to get out of bed and get started. I'll see you later, okay?"

"Right. Take care."

"Bye." She hung up the phone, took a shower, and got dressed. The nightmare from last night had retreated far into her memory. It was always the case, Charlie counseled herself, that whenever something wonderful happened, there was usually some sort of letdown that followed, sooner or later.

She drove straight to the Medical Examiner's office, and found her way to the suite where Bryan's office was located. The grim-faced receptionist informed Charlie that

Dr. Stone was there, but had left instructions not to be disturbed.

Charlie looked at her with immense pity. This poor girl must be desperate for money to work for such an ogre as Bryan Stone. To bluster at her would be a sin, she decided.

"Could you please let him know that Dr. Charlene Warren is here to see him." Charlie said kindly.

The lady picked up the phone receiver and relayed the message to the occupant behind the closed door. "He'll see you now," she said flatly, lowering the receiver to its cradle.

Charlie suddenly felt a twinge of fear running up and down her spine. This is what Grandfather and Angus must have felt during the war when they went into battle. Calming herself with a silent prayer, Charlie entered the room.

Bryan was there behind his desk, sitting with his hands clasped before him. He did not get up when she entered, nor did he offer her a chair. "What can I do for you, Dr. Warren?" he asked coldly.

"I have read your report, Dr. Stone, and it is completely inadequate" her voice was amazingly calm, and Charlie felt a well of peace in her heart which told her that she was there for the right reason, doing the right thing. Jenny Thatcher deserved justice, and it was Charlie's responsibility to make sure that justice happened.

These thoughts emboldened her, so Charlie continued. "Your report, other than being a verbatim transcript of my external examination findings, completely lacks any sort of toxicological analysis of the remaining organs. There is no summary of the findings, merely a repeat of your initial assessment. This report of yours falls far below the minimum standards of forensic science, and would not stand up in court. It is a completely useless document."

Bryan said nothing for a moment. He stared at Charlie, his cold blue eyes darkening abruptly as he gathered himself for a reply. The room became cold and still as he finally spoke. Leaning forward slightly, Bryan said to her, "You find this report inadequate?" he said softly.

His response startled Charlie, who had expected an explosion of outraged bombast. "Completely," she replied steadily.

"Dr. Warren, I was instructed by my superiors to extend you the professional courtesy of assisting with my examination of Jenny Thatcher's remains," Bryan said, his voice coming out in slow, stone-like syllables. "I extended that courtesy, and you proceeded to put on a display of temper that was unworthy of a first year medical student. You badger my office into releasing this report, and then you turn around and tell me that it is inadequate. Finally, you come into my office, uninvited and accuse me of gross negligence."

"No sir," Charlie clarified, "Not negligence: incompetence."

Bryan rose from his chair. "I find your manner to be personally insulting, and your professional conduct to be reprehensible. I do not know the laws that govern slander in the United Kingdom, but your words to me in this office could be actionable." Cold fury gripped his voice. "You will leave my office, and not come back. I plan on lodging a complaint with your superiors at the British Consulate, as well as the State Department. Ideally, they will recall your visa and you will be sent out of this country as soon as possible."

A deadly cold filled the room as he spoke these words. Charlie felt it folding over her like a death shroud, freezing her very soul. She realized that Bryan Stone was evil, purely evil. Knowing this gave Charlie courage to face her enemy. Walking to his desk, she slammed his report down onto the surface.

"So be it," she said with courage and triumph in her voice.

Bryan stared at the report for a minute, then looked up. "In ancient times, when a knight threw his mailed gauntlet down in front of an adversary, the action was considered a challenge to single combat. Are you challenging me, Dr. Warren?" His voice dropped to a malevolent whisper.

"Pick up your report, Dr. Stone," Charlene Warren said coldly. Bryan slowly picked it up.

"To the death, Dr. Warren?" Bryan's question rippled with malevolence, and fury. His eyes glanced down to the Celtic cross around her neck. Gazing almost fixedly at it, his face contorted for a millisecond in unbelievable rage.

"You have said it," Charlie replied, standing straight and proud.

"Then that is how it shall be," replied Bryan, clenching the report like a drawn sword. "You pathetic little guttersnipe. I will break you in two with my bare hands before this is over. You will kneel before me, Warren, and you will plead for mercy, I swear it."

She turned on her heel without replying to him and left the room, leaving Bryan sputtering with rage. Charlie managed to leave the building before what had happened caught up with her. A rush of overwhelming weakness seized her body, causing her to nearly fall against her car. Opening the door, Charlie stepped in and leaned against the steering wheel, waiting for strength to return. The encounter with Bryan had been the most exhausting experience of her life. During the encounter, Charlie had the strangest feeling that her conversation had been proceeding on two levels. While she was talking to him on one level, another part of her was somehow addressing him on some other, deeper level. Charlie's very presence in the office was somehow a violent and direct challenge to his being.

Finally, Charlie had enough strength to call David. "I've been to Bryan's office," she said weakly.

"Charlie, you sound terrible. What happened in there?" his voice radiated concern. "Do you need me to come get you? Are you sick?"

"No, I'm fine," Charlie whispered. "It's so good to just hear your voice right now. I'm getting my strength back. Just keep on talking to me while I rest."

David gave her a rundown on the events of the day. Joan wanted to schedule a department briefing for the afternoon to give everyone an idea on where the case was.

Charlie realized that it was time to put things together. "I think that's a good idea, David," her voice finally recovering to allow her to speak normally. "I think we are ready to tell the world what we know."

"Are you coming to the station now?"

"No," said Charlie. "I need to stop by Trinity for a moment to see Angus." A strange and terrible fear for his safety had suddenly gripped her mind.

"Give him my love, and thank him again for last night." David said.

"I will, Bye." she hung up the phone and drove to Trinity. Without knowing why, Charlie ran up to the rectory door and noticed it was open.

"Uncle Angus?" she called as she went through the door. Then she saw his body sprawled across the floor. Charlie sprang to his side and turned him over.

Angus McKendrick's body was ashen gray. He had stopped breathing, Charlie's clinical instincts took over as she opened his mouth and listened for the escape of air. There was none. She breathed into his mouth and felt for a pulse. It was there, weak and thready.

She dialed 911, summoning an ambulance. Angus had started breathing by this time, spontaneously but erratically. He clutched his chest in agony, breathing in gasps.

"Charlie, my lass, I'm so sorry," gasped Angus, His face ran with cold sweat.

Charlie cradled his head in her lap, calming him, even as her own heart was beating out of control. "Lie still, Uncle Angus," she soothed, wiping the sweat from his face. Charlie heard the sirens of the approaching ambulance drawing nearer. "Help is on the way," she kissed his death-cold forehead. Angus smiled up at her.

"I'm at least glad that you're here right now," Angus said in a whisper.

"That's all right, Angus" Charlie said, trying desperately to remain calm and clinical even as her heart was screaming inside of her. "The ambulance is here." The EMT's clattered up to the door with the stretcher. "In here," she called. "He's eighty years old, and just had an MI a few days ago."

"We know," one of the medics said, grief and concern registering on her face. "Father McKendrick is a personal friend of mine. We'll take good care of him."

"I know you will," replied Charlie "Is there anything I can do to help?"

"What happened?" the other medic asked as they loaded Angus onto the stretcher after attaching the leads from the monitor to Angus.

"I found him lying on the floor, not breathing. I turned him over and gave him mouth-to-mouth. He had a pulse, and started breathing spontaneously." She glanced at the rhythm on the monitor. "You need to get him to the hospital right away. May I follow in my car?"

"Of course," replied one of the medics as they raised the stretcher up to transport Angus to the waiting ambulance. They rushed out the door of the rectory.

Charlie closed the door behind her and dialed David. "David: this is Charlie. I came to the rectory and found Angus on the floor. He's having another heart attack. I'm going to the hospital now."

"Of course,' David replied. "What can I do for you?"

"A few prayers would help right now," Charlie's voice broke.

"I'll meet you at the ER." he hung up. David looked up at Joan Richards.

"Why are you looking at me? Get out of here!" Joan almost screamed at him as he rushed out the door. Joan had grown to love Charlie in the short amount of time that she'd known her. She hated crying in front of people, but she could not help the tears of sympathy she felt for Angus and Charlie.

Carl came out of the office. "What's going on?"

Joan quickly brushed aside the offending tears and steadied her voice. "Angus just had another heart attack. Charlie found him and David's on his way to the hospital."

Carl observed Joan's tear-streaked face. "She got under your skin too, huh?" Joan mutely nodded.

"I've known her less than a week, and I already feel about her the way I do my own kids. It's ridiculous," Joan tried to get herself back under control.

Carl nodded slowly, "Yeah, ridiculous." he turned and went back into his office.

David's car beat Charlie and the ambulance to the hospital. As he drove to the hospital, David's heart was filled alternately with rage at his brother, and concern for Angus and Charlie. He got out of his car and raced to the ER entrance just as the ambulance pulled up with Charlie's car right behind it.

"How's he doing?" David asked as Charlie got out of her car. Her tear-streaked face answered his question wordlessly. David gave her a quick hug and then turned his attention to Angus, a wave of fear crossing his heart as he looked into the gray face of the man on the stretcher.

"Let's get him inside," the paramedic said in a flat, commanding tone. The medics wheeled Angus into the ER with Charlie and David right behind. Charlie talked briefly with the ER physician while Angus was moved into a treatment bay. The ER nurse handed him an EKG, which he read swiftly and decided on a course of treatment.

"I can save his heart if we start thrombolytic therapy now. He's listed you as next-of-kin. Do you agree with that course of treatment?"

"Of course, doctor," Charlie said, "Now I'm going to get out of your hair and let you and your people get to work." She went with David out to the waiting room.

David went outside briefly with his cell phone to talk to Carl and give him an update on everything. It was hard for Charlie to leave Angus, but she knew he was in capable hands. Charlie did not throw her weight around when it came to professional matters; she was bright enough to realize that sort of behavior rarely produced anything but poor results and bad feelings. She stayed in the waiting room like all the other worried family members, and let the experts do their jobs.

David came back from outside into the waiting room, and sat next to Charlie on one of the hard plastic chairs. He tentatively put his arm around her shoulder, and she drew close to him.

"I'm so sorry this happened, Charlie," David said. "I don't know what else to say to you right now." She leaned her head on his shoulder. They sat and waited, as people do in ER waiting rooms. People and families came and went, and they still waited. Charlie eventually went to sleep on David's shoulder.

At last, one of the ER staff came for them. Charlie woke up and stretched.

"How long have I been asleep?"

David shrugged. "I don't know. I've been doing duty as your pillow for the past few hours." He stood up and rubbed his back. "Whoever designed these chairs graduated from the Marquis De

Sade School of design. How did you learn to sleep in a place like this?"

"My third year of medical school." answered Charlie. "It was the only place to sleep, sometimes. It feels strange being on the other side of the Emergency Room as one of the patient's relatives waiting for news." She got up and threw her arms around him. "Thanks for being here," Charlie said, kissing him. Her kiss of gratitude surprised him. David felt that it was a generous reward for very little work on his part.

They were brought back to a small room, and the doctor came in. "I think we started treatment in time. His heart seems to be uninjured, but we won't know for sure until a few days from now. He'll be spending a day or so in the ICU, and our cardiologist will want to do a heart catheterization."

"I was expecting that," Charlie said. "Thank you for everything," she added gratefully.

"You know, it's sometimes very intimidating for our staff to treat family members of medical people," the ER doctor confided. "Lots of people like to throw their weight around. You didn't, and believe me, it's appreciated."

Charlie put out her hand. "No, Doctor, I appreciate you and your staff. This is not my bailiwick. You're the expert. Anybody with half a brain should realize that, and respect that."

"You would be amazed at the number of people who do not share your feelings. He'll be ready to go upstairs in a few minutes," the doctor continued. "You can come back now and see him for a moment or two, if you'd like." He showed them the back entrance to the treatment area.

Angus looked much better than he did a few hours ago. He was awake, and he reached up to her with his hands and stroked her face. "Thank you, Charlie, for saving my life." Charlie said nothing. She held his hand next to her face while tears ran down her cheeks.

She bent over him and kissed his forehead. "You saved my life a few months ago, remember? Returning the favor is such a small thing compared to what you did for me."

Angus smiled. He saw David, who was standing back, trying to allow them some privacy. Angus motioned for him to come to the stretcher. David bent down next to him, Angus pulled him closer, and whispered in a voice only he could hear, "David, he wants to kill her. Please protect my Charlie. She may seem tough, and she is in some ways, but she needs you right now."

David nodded and squeezed his hand lightly. "You know I will."

They wheeled Angus up to the ICU. They found out which room he was staying in, and that Stacey Michaels was going to be his nurse for the night.

"Angus is in the hands of the best nurse in the hospital," David said to Charlie in the presence of Ms. Michaels, who blushed furiously at the compliment.

As they left the ICU, James Rosson met them in the waiting room. James hugged Charlie and told her how sorry he was for her and Angus. "You've had a bad day all around, old girl," he said, squeezing her to his side. "Jane's with the kids, otherwise she'd be down here as well. You know what a mother hen she is."

"Oh, I nearly forgot," he said, looking in his coat pocket. " I have some messages for you, since you're Angus' next-of-kin." He produced a very official envelope. "This came by special dispatch."

Charlie looked at it. "This is from Buckingham Palace. I don't understand." She opened the letter. It was an official expression of concern and prayers for Angus' recovery from the Queen. "It's lovely," she said after reading the note, "but I still don't understand why Angus is getting a note like this from the Queen."

James smiled slightly. "Your dear godfather was hiding a very big light under a large bushel, my love. Did you not know that he is a Knight Commander of the Bath?"

Charlie was completely bewildered, "No, I didn't."

James went on: "Then you probably don't know that he also is a recipient of the Victoria Cross as well. That and a handful of other medals the old boy has probably never bothered to tell anyone about. Those things don't mean much in America, but they do overseas, and even though your godfather is a citizen of the United States, in the eyes of Britain, he is a knight of the Realm, and will be as long as he lives."

"I'm not surprised," David said quietly, "not one bit. The real heroes aren't the ones who go around showing off their medals.

The quiet ones, the real heroes like Angus McKendrick, serve their country, and then they move on. That's the way they are, and that's Angus, period."

Charlie nodded. "Angus mounted a volunteer effort from his church after 9/11. They went down for a whole week, ministering to the people helping to clean up that awful mess at the World Trade Center. Angus told me that some of those people saw things that they'd never get over, that it was worse than the Blitz. It was his way of helping out. That's just the way he is."

Carl Davis came into the ICU waiting room. He introduced himself to James Rosson, and turned to David and Charlie. "Okay, sports fans, here's the game plan," he pointed to Charlie. "You are coming with me to my house for the night," James nodded his approval. Carl turned to David: "You are going with James, and then home for the night."

David and Charlie said in unison, "don't we have a say in any of this?"

"No." James and Carl replied simultaneously.

"I know what this is," David said, "this is your thinly disguised attempt to get a break from your three kids beating you up every night. You're throwing Charlie at them."

Carl laughed. "I guess I can't keep secrets from you, can I? Really, Charlie, you don't need to spend the night alone, and you are NOT going to spend it here in the ICU. Do you hear me?"

"Carl is right, Charlie," James added. "Angus would not be happy with you if he found out you'd spent the night outside his door on his account."

Charlie finally relented. "I see what you mean," she said reluctantly. "I'll need to stop by my room and pick up a few things." She stood up and looked at David. "I need to see you out in the hallway for a moment."

She and David went out into the hallway. She took his hand and drew him over to an alcove.

Charlie threw her arms around him and kissed him very thoroughly. "I love you," she said, holding him tightly.

David held her close, stroking her hair. "I love you too." He kissed her again.

Charlie looked up at him. "You've been an angel through all of this," she said. "You've given me everything I've asked of you, and so much more. Please be patient with me."

Carl and James came out into the hallway. They didn't seem the least bit surprised. "Okay you two, time to break it up," Carl said, smiling from ear-to-ear.

"My wife and kids haven't seen you in ages, so let's get going." He took Charlie in tow and started down the hallway. She turned and looked over her shoulder and smiled at David as they disappeared into the elevator.

David looked at the elevator longingly. "How in the name of Heaven did I ever get so lucky?" He shook his head in disbelief.

'These things don't happen by accident, David,' James said with quiet authority. "You needed someone like Charlie, and she needed someone like you. So there you are: God has a way of working these things out." He shook David's hand. "I want you to know how much it's meant to all of us at the Consulate that Charlie has had someone like you to rely upon."

David was embarrassed. "I don't think I've done anything special."

James was insistent. "You're being entirely too modest, my friend. Charlie has no living relatives left in Britain. Other than Angus, Charlie's quite alone in the world."

"No James, that's not true," David said. "She has you and your family, she has Carl and his family, and probably dozens of others that you or I know nothing about. Charlie is the sort that is never alone in this world. She may not have any blood relatives, but she will always have a family. Charlie is one of those special people in the world who creates families wherever they go."

"She also has you, my friend." James said. "Charlie is like a little sister to me, David. She nearly went insane after her brother and grandfather died. Angus came over from America to be with her for a while. Charlie's only been really well for the last few months. She took medical leave from her teaching post at Bramshill for a while to get back on her feet."

David was amazed. "You'd never know it by the way she acts that she's been through so much. She's so happy and alive."

"Well that's where you come in, old boy," James said warmly. "That's your doing. We have you to thank for that. You've given us back our old Charlie. You brought her back to life."

David looked embarrassed as James said all of this. "I think that's a little overstated James. I'm just a regular guy who happens to be crazy about her, that's all."

Well, let me conclude my little sermon to you with this fact: Charlie could have been married a dozen times over by now, but she hasn't been interested. No one has ever come close, until you showed up. Charlie loves you, and I know you love her. Don't worry about the window dressing; all of the details will get sorted out. Trust me in that."

"I hope so, James. You know I lost my wife Karen a few months ago. She died in this hospital."

"Yes, I know that, David," James said. "Carl talked to me about you when we knew Charlie was coming over. Please do not think we have been involved in some sort of matchmaking situation. What has happened between you and Charlie has been your business and your doing, not ours. I will say that everyone is pleased that two wonderful people like you have come together in such a marvelous way."

They were still standing in the hallway, having this conversation. David was suddenly aware that it was almost evening. "Excuse me, James, but would you like to go somewhere and have dinner? I've been summarily dismissed from my responsibility of caring for Charlie, at least for the night."

James laughed, "It's just a temporary dismissal, David. But no, thank you, I have to get home to my family now. You are planning to come for the party at the Consulate on Saturday, aren't you?"

"Well, I guess so, if Charlie's up to it."

"Let's hope so." James said. "Well, it was good to see you again." He walked down the hallway to the elevator with David. They took the elevator to the ground floor. When they got off the elevator, James remembered something, and he turned to David.

"David, I need to let you know something. Your brother has lodged a formal protest with the Consulate concerning Charlie.

He's also contacted the State Department as well. For obvious reasons, I didn't say anything to Charlie tonight about it."

"Is this something to worry about?" David asked.

James thought for a moment. "It could be, but I'll do what I can to take care of it. Your brother has made things difficult for her."

A cold fury rose inside of David. "If my brother has said or done anything to hurt Charlie, I swear to you that I will personally take it out of his hide."

James held up a cautioning hand. "I understand how you feel. If you give in to your completely understandable desire to take this out personally on Bryan, you will play into his hands. I daresay he would welcome it," He added grimly. "Trust me, when it comes to Charlie Warren, the man who tries to harm her will die at my hands. I swear it as an officer of Her Majesty's SAS."

"So what do we do?" David asked with frustrated anger in his voice.

"Well, first off, Charlie Warren is a very smart girl." James said with pride. "She mailed off a copy of Bryan's report along with her official critique to his superiors. As a member of the investigating team, she had the right to ask for a second look at that report. They were completely aware of her intention to go down to the Medical Examiner's office today. Everything was above board and in the open. Bryan obviously thought that he was dealing with some sort of hysterical female. He most certainly was not."

David laughed. "I think that anybody who underestimates Charlie Warren is a complete fool."

"I agree with you, David," James replied. "But just think about this for a moment: if you simply looked at her, and didn't know anything about her, she looks like a little schoolgirl, doesn't she? Charlie has a very sweet and outgoing disposition, and most people do not associate such things with someone with a brilliant and dynamic mind."

"I have to confess, James, that I felt that way when I first met her. Charlie set me straight in short order."

James smiled understandingly. "I'm sure she did, David. Charlie does not suffer fools lightly. The fact that she finds you interesting enough and worthy enough to have a personal relationship with her says a lot about you as well.

"Well, I don't know about that. I just think she's terrific. I also sense from what you've said to me that people have underestimated Charlie before, to their everlasting regret," David observed.

"Yes, they have," laughed James. "She's so disarming, you know: looks all sweet and innocent, and then the trap closes on them before they're even aware they're in trouble."

"That's good to know. Now I can sleep better. Good night, James."

They shook hands as they left the hospital. David drove to his house, and attempted to go to sleep. He finally did, after much tossing and turning.

Charlie left the hospital in her car, stopping by to pick up some items and a change of clothing. Carl followed her in his car, waited until she was finished, and then drove her to his home. He called ahead and let his wife know they were coming.

Sarah was used to this sort of thing. Carl usually had friends over at last a few times every week. She told her kids that Aunt Charlie was coming to spend the night with them.

It was a mistake. Charlie was promptly attacked the moment she came through the door. For the next ten minutes, there was a pile consisting of Charlie and three screaming, giggling children blocking the entryway. Carl noted this with satisfaction and entered the house through the back door.

Sarah finally had to restore order. "Hey!" she yelled at Charlie, "You're worse than my kids! Get up off of that floor and give me a hug!"

Charlie finally untangled herself from the kids, stood up and gave Sarah a big hug.

"Oh darling, it's so good to see you again!" Sarah said. "I heard about Angus. I'm so sorry."

"That's all right, Sarah," Charlie said. "You can thank your husband for the disruption in your household."

"Disruption? What are you talking about? This sort of thing goes on all the time around this place. Your reception was tame compared to what Carl gets when he comes home." Sarah directed her attention to her three offspring. "All of you go out and get Aunt Charlie's bags. Then come back inside and wash up for dinner. AND DON'T SLAM THE DOOR!!!" This last comment occurred a millisecond after the door crashed shut.

Charlie looked at Sarah and grinned. It was so good to be around people who were openly loving and affectionate. This was exactly where she needed to be right now.

"Is there anything I could help you with, Sarah?" she asked as Sarah busied herself around the kitchen.

"Yes, you can go see if my little heathens have washed their hands and have started to set my table." Sarah replied. Charlie went out and helped the children set the table, which was slightly less noisy and chaotic than the previous scene in the entryway. Carl arrived just in time after changing his clothes to restore some sort of order to the setting of the table.

Sarah came in with the food, in quantities more than enough to feed her family. "I always fix more, because the night watch usually shows up here around ten or so begging for food," she explained.

They all sat down, joined hands and prayed. Carl thanked God for the food, for Charlie, and for strength and health for Angus McKendrick. The silence in the house lasted throughout the prayer, but not one second more.

Supper consisted of food, laughs, more food, and lots of noise from everyone. Carl and Sarah deeply loved each other, and they loved their kids. For all the noise and bedlam, their kids were very well behaved, except when Carl was home or when Charlie came to visit.

Supper was finally over, and Carl and the kids cleared the table, leaving Charlie and Sarah to actually have a few moments together over some coffee.

Sarah reached over and put her hand on top of Charlie's. "You look good, sweetheart, better than I've seen you look in a good long while. Carl's been telling me that you and David hit it off really well."

Charlie blushed, "It's so unexpected. I mean I didn't come over here from England to fall in love. It just happened that way."

"Well honey, I didn't go to church to fall in love either. But that's what happened with Carl and me. That man never knew what hit him. He still doesn't" Sarah chuckled softly.

"Let me guess, Charlie. She's out there telling you about church and how I didn't know what hit me, right?" Carl chimed in from the kitchen.

"Leave me out of this," Charlie said.

"Carl Davis, don't make me come in there and straighten you out, because you know I can, and will."

"The Voice has spoken," Carl intoned.

"I think you're officially in trouble now, Carl," observed Charlie. "I guess I'm going upstairs now for bedtime stories and prayers." She went up the stairs to the kid's rooms. While she was upstairs, Carl came up to Sarah, put his arm around her waist, and kissed her neck.

"She seems really happy, Carl." Sarah said, looking up the stairwell to the kids' rooms, which were full of noisy, happy sounds.

"I think she is," Carl replied. "I know David's much happier now that Charlie's around."

"Do you think there's a chance that she might consider settling down here in Compton?" Sarah asked hopefully. Charlie had been "adopted" by them when she was down at the Academy with Carl. She was giving a voice to something both Carl and she had always wanted to happen.

"I don't know," Carl said. "It depends on a lot of things, mostly what she and David plan on doing with the way they feel about each other."

The noise from upstairs had finally died down. Charlie came downstairs with a big grin on her face.

"They've all grown so much, I just can't believe it." Charlie said.

"Kids get that way, Charlie," observed Carl sagely. Both women looked at him as though he had just grown two heads.

"More wisdom from the expert," Sarah said, arching her eyebrows. "Charlie, he's the biggest kid of them all, and that's the truth."

Charlie put her arms around him. "I think he's a love."

Carl basked in momentary glory. "See Sarah? I'm a love."

"Well, it's almost time for the grownups to go to bed. You too, Carl." Sarah said, guiding Charlie to the guest room on the ground floor. "You know where everything is, and there are new sheets on the bed, so you're all set."

"I imagine that you'll want to go to the hospital tomorrow morning, Charlie."

Carl said. "Do you want to sleep in tomorrow, or get up with the rest of the family?"

"I doubt if I'll sleep past the time the children get up," predicted Charlie.

There was a thunderstorm that night. Standard operating procedure in the Davis household dictated that all the kids piled into Carl and Sarah's bed at the first sound of thunder. Charlie's presence changed all that, and about two hours later, she wound up with three small visitors who crawled into her bed. An impromptu slumber party ensued, finally ending sometime after one in the morning when everyone fell asleep.

Charlie didn't mind one bit. Being in Carl's home brought back memories of her parent's home back in England when she was a child. With those pleasant memories drifting through her head, she floated off into a pleasant, peaceful sleep.

6

Charlie woke up at six thirty feeling refreshed and alive. She did this even though the bed was taken up by three other small sleeping occupants. Her stirrings woke them up, which precipitated another ten-minute pillow fight. Their noises woke up Carl and Sarah, who weren't the least bit surprised by what they heard and found in their guest room. Sarah shooed the kids off to their respective rooms to get dressed and out the door to play after breakfast.

She came into Charlie's room bearing two cups of coffee. Sarah gave one to Charlie and sat down on the bed.

"Thank you for having me over, Sarah," Charlie said with gratitude in her voice. "I've missed the sounds of children and family so much. It's like beautiful music."

"Maybe the time has come for you to make your own music, Charlie," Sarah said quietly. Charlie blushed. Sarah put her hand out on top of Charlie's. "I'm not trying to pry into your life. I know things are complicated right now, but sometimes having someone else to help you figure things out is a good thing."

Charlie nodded and smiled. "You and Carl are so good for each other. I could only hope and pray that something like that will happen for me."

Sarah smiled at Charlie and hugged her. "Perhaps sooner than you think. Now I have to get my family ready. The kids and Carl are making breakfast, and Heaven knows what they're doing to my kitchen." She hurried out of the room.

Charlie showered and dressed quickly. She sat down to breakfast and ate quietly. Carl and Sarah knew she wanted to get down to the hospital as soon as possible.

There was a knock on the back door. It was David. "I'm your chauffer for the day, milady," he said in a mock British accent.

Charlie threw a muffin at him, "Carl, make him stop. He's making fun of me!"

David caught the muffin in midair and started eating it. "Sarah, don't you have rules about people throwing food in your house?"

"Yes, Dave, I do," replied Sarah, "I also have rules about people badgering my guests."

"I think Charlie can take care of herself, can't you, Charlie?" Carl said. Turning to David, he winked broadly. "Your responsibility today is to make sure this girl stays out of trouble, okay?"

"Yeah, right, like that's really going to happen" said David. "Let's go see Angus, Charlie."

Charlie rose from the chair and hugged Carl and Sarah. "Thanks again for everything. We're going now, so your children aren't exposed to what's going to happen to David for his remarks!"

"You know where we are, Charlie. The door's always open." Sarah said.

Charlie and David went out to his car. "You are such a beast!" she said, playfully punching his arm. She threw her arms around him. "I missed you so much last night," she said softly, kissing him.

David kissed her back and held her close. "I'm getting used to having you around too, you know."

"I'm getting rather used to having you around as well," responded Charlie, rewarding him with a brilliant smile.

"You've made a big difference in my life, Charlie," David hand her hand and brought it to his lips, kissing it. "You are a kind, gentle, brave young lady."

Charlie bowed her head. She was accustomed to men trying to flatter her or pick her up. David's words, and his kind, gentle way of treating her, was completely different from anything she had experienced before. He honored her, and she knew that he meant every word. "Let's get over to the hospital to see Angus." she finally said.

They drove over to the hospital. When they got to the ICU, they found that Angus had already been sent to the catheterization lab for his angiogram. There were some people from Trinity Church in the Waiting Room.

"Dr. Warren, I'm Steven Morton, the head of the parish council," A tall, distinguished looking man came up to Charlie, shaking her hand. "We have a rather extraordinary request to ask of you." He glanced around nervously.

"What is it, Mr. Morton? What can I do to help you and your church?" Charlie said, trying to put the man at ease. The other church members came up and stood next to Mr. Morton.

"Well, Dr. Warren, Angus told us some time ago that he had a goddaughter in Britain who was not only a doctor and a forensic investigator, but also an ordained deacon in the Anglican Church."

"That's right, I am an ordained deacon," Charlie admitted reluctantly. Now it was her turn to get nervous.

"Well, here's the problem, Doctor," one of the ladies said, "tomorrow is Sunday. We have no minister in our church to conduct the service, and no deacon to assist or step into Angus' shoes when he's sick. Trinity is a very small church, and we have very little resources. Our diocese is short of ministers of any sort to begin with."

Mr. Morton pressed on: "Since you are an ordained deacon, we were wondering if you would come to Trinity tomorrow and lead our worship service."

"We've already cleared it with the diocese office. They said that would be fine," chimed in another one of the ladies in a bright, cheerful voice.

"I see someone else is been hiding lights under bushels besides Uncle Angus," murmured David, who was standing close to Charlie. His remark earned him a sharp poke in the ribs.

Charlie looked at their hopeful faces. They had come to her for help. Charlie knew she could not let them down, despite her own feelings of complete and total inadequacy. She took a deep breath, and said words that she dreaded to say: "I will come and conduct your service, my friends. I will need your help, because I have never done anything like this by myself before. We will have

Morning Prayer, not Communion. I do not feel comfortable serving the Eucharist in my godfather's church."

The little group brightened up considerably when they heard Charlie speak. "Thank you so much for helping, Dr. Warren. Angus told us you were a wonderful person. We'll be looking forward to seeing you. We've been praying for you for many months now." Mr. Morton said, taking her hand again. "Our service starts at nine. We'll give you all the help we can."

He handed her a set of keys. "I talked to Angus before he went to the cath lab, and he told me to give you these. These are the keys to the church, and the rectory, in case you need anything."

"Dr. Warren, since you are here, right now, would you lead us in prayer for Angus?" one of the ladies asked.

"Of course," Charlie said, bowing her head. Everyone in the room became silent, and Charlie prayed for Angus and his quick recovery, and for his church.

"Well, we will see you tomorrow then," Mr. Morton said, shaking her hand. "Thank you again, Dr. Warren."

Charlie thanked them all, and managed to smile as the little group left the waiting room. When she and David were left in the room by themselves, Charlie turned around to David and put her head on his shoulder.

"Help," she said in a small voice.

David looked at her, alarmed at her appearance. Charlie looked as though she was about to faint. "What can I do to help you, Charlie?" he said, with deep concern in his voice.

Charlie sat down in a chair with her head in her hands. "I don't know, David. I was ordained a number of years ago in my home parish to help our local minister out. Most of the cathedrals in Britain are nothing more than large museums, David. England has many wonderful houses of worship but very few practicing ministers. We need more, many more people to minister to our people, but few men and women come forward to do that task. Some respond to the call, but they are stretched thin, and they need all the help they can get. That is why I volunteered to help them out.

"I would never willingly agree to conduct a service, unless it was an emergency. Well, I've come to America, and an emergency has occurred. What else can I do? Say 'no' to them?"

"You already know the answer to your question, Charlie." David said with quiet confidence. "God will give you what you need to help these people. That's what you do: step up and help, just like your uncle and the rest of your family."

Charlie reached up and took his hand. "David, I'm so glad you're here to help me with this. I couldn't do something like this without your help."

Stacey Michaels came into the room, along with the cardiologist. He came to Dr. Warren and shook her hand. "Dr. Warren, I'm so glad to finally meet you. Stacey has been telling me about you and David here," the doctor said warmly.

"Thank you, Doctor," Charlie said, blushing, "but I'm not all that special," she shot a warning glance at David, telling him to shut up. David shut up. "How is Angus?" she asked.

"Well, he's fine, thanks to you," the cardiologist continued. "His heart vessels are amazingly clean, and I don't think he'll have any further trouble. I'll be releasing Father McKendrick on Monday, perhaps even earlier if he does especially well. By the way, I'm looking forward to the service tomorrow." He smiled at them and Stacey, and left the room.

"I'll take you to Angus now, if you'd like," Stacey said, leading them back into the ICU. Angus was back in his room after the heart cath. He lay straight in bed with a sandbag on his right leg where the catheter had been inserted. Despite all of the things he had undergone that day, Angus looked much better than yesterday.

Charlie bent over the bed and kissed him. "I'm so glad you're better, and I'm so angry with you." Angus knew exactly what she was talking about.

"They told you what they wanted, didn't they?" Angus asked. Charlie nodded. "You said 'yes', didn't you?" Charlie nodded again.

Angus sighed. "Dearest, it was not my idea, but in a way, I'm glad. I know you will be able to do this."

"That makes one of us. They gave me the keys to the church, Uncle Angus. They trusted me with the keys. Why did they do that?" Charlie asked with wonder in her voice.

"They believe in you," he replied. "Besides, you need to have some materials to prepare your sermon tomorrow. My library is at your disposal."

"Well, I can see that today has been planned out for us," David said cheerfully. "Charlie needs to go to the rectory to prepare her sermon, and then tonight, I get to take Cinderella to the ball. By the way, where does one carry a nine-millimeter Glock while wearing an evening dress?" David said these things to get Charlie out of the emotional tailspin she was in. It worked. Charlie wrinkled her nose and stuck out her tongue at him.

"Stacey," Charlie impishly called to Ms Michaels who just entered the room to take Angus' vital signs. "Are there any more ICU beds open? You might have a trauma case come in shortly." She glared at David, who smiled back beatifically.

Stacey and Angus both laughed. "You two need to leave now," Stacey said to Charlie and David. "I'll take good care of Angus for you."

"We know you will." Charlie said. Leaving the ICU with David, they went down to David's car.

"Seriously, Charlie," David said, "I know that was something completely unexpected, and I didn't mean to make things harder for you."

Charlie reached over and kissed him. "You dear sweet man, you did nothing of the sort. I enjoy it when you tease me, just remember that I tease back," she added impishly. David responded by kissing her again.

They got into the car and drove back to Carl's house to pick up Charlie's things. David looked at his watch. "By the way, what time is this thing tonight at the Consulate?"

"I don't recall James giving a time," replied Charlie. "I'll ring him up and find out." She dialed up James' home phone number and got Jane on the line. "Hello? Jane, it's so good to hear your voice! What? Yes, he's doing much better, thank you. Is James around? Do you know what time this dinner is at the Consulate?

Oh, six. Yes I'll be there. Yes, he's coming too. What? Yes, he is rather a love, even if he is an American." David winked at her and she made a face at him as she said this. "Okay, I'll see you then. Bye."

David made some quick calculations. "That gives you about five to six hours to come up with a sermon. I'm going to drop you off at the Rectory and go down to the station. We lost some time yesterday."

They pulled into the Davis' driveway. Charlie got out and went inside to get her clothes and other items. She reemerged after about ten minutes, laughing at the door, and saying, "I'll see you tomorrow, Sarah." Charlie came back to the car and climbed in.

David drove her to the Rectory and let her off at the door. Charlie leaned over before she got out of the car. "I love you so much. Believe me when I tell you I couldn't be able to do what I'm going to be doing on Sunday if it weren't for you. You've been so wonderful and supportive of me. Pick me up around four-thirty."

"Okay," he kissed her again. "I'll see you later." He drove off to the station, leaving Charlie at the doorstep.

Charlie turned the key in the lock and went inside. It seemed strange to be in Angus' rectory without him. The books in the front parlor gave off a comfortable smell of old paper and ancient bindings. She looked over the titles, selected some of the commentaries and resources familiar to her, and with a Bible at hand, set to work.

Charlie worked swiftly and efficiently on her sermon. The message came together astonishingly fast. Considering the horrific events of the past few days, it was not difficult for her to come up with a topic.

As she worked on her sermon, Charlie's thoughts kept turning to Bryan and his odd behavior. Something was deeply wrong with him. It was not just narcissism or an malignant sense of pride. Bryan's manner and presence was unnatural, almost as if something or someone was controlling his body and mind. Charlie's concerns about him intensified as the afternoon progressed. After she completed the sermon, and was satisfied with its final form, Charlie decided to do some further research.

As a physician, and as a forensic scientist, Charlie was very familiar with all the myriad manifestations of human psychopathology. Bryan Stone was definitely mentally ill, but he was also more than that. Charlie systematically reviewed in her mind the various categories of mental disorders, which could describe or fit the things that she had seen or suspected when she had encountered Bryan Stone.

She reviewed the various puzzling aspects of the case: the threatening message addressed to her written in contemporary ink on contemporary paper which matched hundred-year old samples of Jack the Ripper's handwriting, the problem of Jenny Thatcher's body lifted up onto a cross suspended nine feet over the altar, the desecration of the church itself, and the attacks on Angus McKendrick. David had told her about Stacey Michael's encounter with the apparition which walked through the wall in the ICU. Angus had told her that he had seen it as well; it was not a hallucination. Charlie thought of her own experience in her hotel room that night before Angus had his heart attack. All of these things bespoke a pattern of intelligence and attack that was supernatural and malevolent in origin.

Charlie got up from her godfather's desk where she had been working and went over and searched through the rows of books. It was some time before Charlie's search yielded results, but she found a few titles under the subject she was interested in.

Charlie's suspicions were confirmed after a few more hours of careful study of the texts she selected. It would be difficult for her to confide her suspicions to David without more data. David was a trained investigator who did not jump to conclusions. He would resist Charlie's conclusions unless there was definite proof. Charlie had excluded every avenue other than the one that pointed to the conclusion that the evidence supported.

Her conclusion was that Bryan Stone was demonically possessed.

At the police station, David was also thinking about his brother. Bryan had always been a boor, but the idea that he would threaten someone like Charlie Warren enraged David. The temptation to drive to Bryan's home and physically confront him was almost overwhelming. He resisted the impulse with a supreme effort, forcing himself to be professional. While thrashing his brother would be psychologically rewarding for a few moments, it would destroy his career as a police officer.

Then there was Charlie. She had flooded his world with light, goodness, and grace. David's life seemed to be opening up to new and wonderful people and ideas. Charlie was responsible for this awakening, and he never wanted her to leave his side ever again.

David arrived at the police station, much to the surprise of the officers manning the weekend duty watch, and went straight to work. Joan Richard's team had gotten an excellent casting from the tire tracks left at the cab location. They matched a late model mini-van, and the team was now running down in-state purchases of vehicles of that sort within the local area. The fiber samples that Charlie found at the church matched carpet used to cover the floors of such vans. Interviews of the farmers and neighbors surrounding the cab site failed to turn up any significant information on abandoned buildings. No one had seen or heard anything unusual the night that Jenny Thatcher had been murdered.

Joan had also reviewed abandoned industrial parks in the area for possible sites, and none existed that would be easily accessible. Charlie postulated from the degree of expertise shown on the injuries inflicted on Jenny Thatcher that the killer would have needed at least two hours to operate on her. That narrowed the driving radius considerably, and once again, the facts pointed to a residence or facility located somewhere in Compton.

The New York City Medical Examiner's report on the organs taken from Jenny Thatcher showed traces of drugs used by anesthesiologists to produce quick unconsciousness, as well as long-acting paralyzing agents. They agreed with Charlie's conclusions that someone with a high degree of medical knowledge had removed the organs from Jenny Thatcher's body.

David swiftly wrote down notes on these findings along with his impressions. He was careful and systematic, not wanting to leave anything unconsidered. He decided that the investigation was shaping up nicely.

Charlie was planning on working on a profile of the killer based on the evidence and her impressions as a forensic investigator. Her analysis, along with the two medical examiner's reports and Joan Richards' crime scene analyses, would be combined together for a presentation of the case to the department on Tuesday.

David was so engrossed in his work that time nearly ran away from him. It was nearly three-thirty when he finally looked at his watch. Suddenly he remembered that he failed to ask Charlie what he should wear to this dinner at the Consulate tonight.

He called the rectory. Charlie answered, "Hello?"

David replied, "You have the most beautiful voice."

Charlie giggled at the other end of the line, "Why thank you, kind sir. What can I do for you?"

"What does one wear to a Consulate dinner?" David asked. "Doublet and hose?"

Charlie snorted, "Of course not, you goose. Let's see: it's not a formal state function, so a nice suit would probably fit the bill."

"And what are you going to be wearing, Cinderella?"

"Oh, I'll think of something," she said dreamily.

"I can't wait to see you. Will four-thirty be soon enough for you?"

"Heavens yes," Charlie replied. "It doesn't take me that long to look presentable. How are things coming along with the case?"

"Just fine," David said, stretching out at his desk. "Actually I'm at a good stopping place. How about you?"

"I need to work on a few more things, so I'll see you at four-thirty."

"Okay, " David said. "I'll see you later. Bye." He hung up the phone, gathered his reports together, and left the building. Driving back to his house, he thought about the last time he and Karen had gone to a formal affair. It seemed ages ago. Karen had been so much like Charlie, David thought: so young and alive and vibrant. It was strange, in a way, that his love for Charlie could coexist so well and harmoniously with his feelings for Karen. It was almost as though the two sets of feelings complemented one another in a unified blend.

David arrived at home and dressed quickly. When the clock showed four- fifteen, he was already in the car backing out of the driveway. His car pulled up at the rectory at four-thirty. Charlie was waiting for him at the door. David got out of the car and went up to the doorstep. "Hi," he said, looking like a high school kid on his first date.

Charlie smiled at him as he came up to her. "My, don't we look handsome," she said, straightening his tie. "I have my work cut out for me to come up to your standards."

He kissed her. "You met and exceeded those standards long ago."

She dimpled at the remark. "Well, let's get me over to the hotel so I can get changed."

David stayed in the hotel lobby. Charlie was down half an hour later. He stood up and turned around when the elevator opened. David's jaw dropped: Charlie looked like a fairy tale princess in a deep burgundy dress. He came up to her and raised her hand to his lips. Kissing it, David murmured, "you look enchanting tonight, my love."

Charlie curtsied lightly. "Thank you," she took his arm. "shall we go to the ball?"

They arrived at the Consulate at five minutes to six. James Rosson and Jane were at the door. They greeted David and Charlie warmly, escorting them to the dining room where Lady Margaret and her husband were waiting. "I'm so glad you could come tonight," the Consul said. "James has told everyone about you, David, and how you've taken Charlie under your wing."

David felt a little awkward at the lavish praise heaped on him. "I really haven't done much, ma'am. Charlie's been a tremendous help to our case. She's a brilliant forensic investigator."

Lady Margaret Wilson beamed at the compliments. "Charlie Warren has always been a bright light in Britain. Her whole family has a long record of distinguished service to the British Crown."

"Yes," David said, smiling at Charlie, "She was telling me about Sir Francis Drake and her ancestor who sailed with him on the *Golden Hind*."

"One of the more distinguished ancestors Dr. Warren can lay claim to." Lady Margaret said. Turning to Charlie, she asked, "How is your heart patient, Dr, Warren?"

"Angus is doing well, ma'am," Charlie said. "His heart catheterization was normal."

"Good for him," replied the Consul with satisfaction in her voice. "I understand you are going to be preaching in his pulpit tomorrow." Charlie blushed at the remark.

"Yes ma'am, the vestry insisted," she said in an embarrassed tone. "I am terrified of the prospect of preaching in his absence."

"Nonsense," retorted Lady Margaret, "you'll do splendidly. I am looking forward to hearing you tomorrow." Charlie blanched and her eyes went wide with fright.

"I will do my best, ma'am," she whispered. Lady Margaret smiled and moved off to her other guests.

James came up to Charlie. "You have Carl to thank for that revelation, darling. He was proud as a peacock when he found out the news. You're going to have your own regular cheering section tomorrow morning."

"Don't you mean hanging party?" groaned Charlie. "I'll be excommunicated, probably."

"The SAS motto is: 'he who dares, wins'. I think you should remember that, my love." James said.

"So far, I haven't seen much that Charlie does where she doesn't succeed," added David. "She actually is a fairly good cook, for a Brit, that is."

"You know, I still haven't shown you what I can do in hand-to-hand, David," Charlie threatened sweetly. "Monday might be a good time for a demonstration."

Everyone laughed. David finally relaxed. These people loved Charlie, and since they had that in common with him, they all got along splendidly.

Jane and Charlie moved over to a quiet corner where they could talk quietly and catch up on all the news. Jane Rosson was a striking woman who was slightly taller than Charlie, and about four years older. She had short, raven-black hair and deep brown, almost black eyes which flashed with energy and intelligence. Charlie told her all about what had happened between her and David. Jane nodded and hugged Charlie once she was finished with her news.

"He really is wonderful, Charlie," said Jane admiringly. "He's also crazy about you."

"I know, Jane, I'm crazy about him, too." Charlie said quietly, watching David laugh and joke with the others. "I can't believe this is happening to me."

"Well, we're all delighted for you," affirmed Jane, squeezing Charlie's hand.

James and David watched Jane and Charlie from across the room. "Sisters," observed James, shaking his head slightly. "They couldn't be more close if they'd been born to the same parents."

David nodded his understanding." What an amazing pair they make. How did Jane and Charlie meet?" he asked.

"They were roommates at Oxford," James told him. "Charlie was fourteen at the time, and Jane just took her under her wing. Jane's family lives close to where Charlie had been brought up, so it wasn't much of a stretch that the two would develop that sort of relationship once they got to University. Jane made sure Charlie was safe, and kept her out of mischief for the most part."

"For the most part, now there's a phrase that says a lot." David laughed. "That little girl is a mischief magnet."

"You do catch on quickly, my friend," laughed James. "Jane is much the same way, so you can gather what happened when the two of them were paired together. They spent several summers as student interns at the Royal Shakespeare Company in Stratford. They studied stage fighting with rapiers and daggers"

"This is a surprise?" David asked mockingly. "Charlie looks great in a dress, but I don't think she's the damsel-in-distress type."

"Neither is Jane," observed James. " They were completely useless as ladies-in-waiting and all of those minor female characters the Bard is so famous for. They were more interested in learning about weapons and stage fighting, which makes perfect sense if you understand their childhoods. They spent most of their time as kids romping around the English countryside slaying dragons and such. England still hasn't recovered." They both laughed.

"I just can't imagine being in college at fourteen," David remarked. "You know, James, she seems so incredibly happy and well adjusted. I had no idea that she was so brilliant."

"That's because she doesn't go throwing it around," James explained. "Charlie wasn't raised to be special or to put on airs. Her parents were very levelheaded about that sort of thing."

"I think they did a remarkable job, James. She's really wonderful." David gazed lovingly across the room at her. Charlie looked up as he did and their eyes met. She smiled slightly and returned to her conversation with Jane. "For some reason I feel as though she's able to predict what I'm going to say or do a microsecond before it happens."

James smiled enigmatically. "Charlie's very in tune with people, David. It's one of her gifts. My Jane is somewhat like that. Believe me, it can be disconcerting at times, but you'll get used to it. A little advice, my friend: don't put her up on a pedestal. She hates that, and she also has a bit of a temper which you may have already noticed."

"Thanks, James." David said with gratitude as the two women came up to them. Charlie gave David a knowing look.

"We can feel our ears burning from across the room, gentlemen. James, what sort of tales have you been telling out of school? You'd better confess, because you know I'll find out, and then you'll have me to deal with, along with Jane."

"Fess up, Tex; we're surrounded." David laughed.

"'*Res ipsa loquitur,*' the thing speaks for itself," laughed James. "I was just telling David how you two have been joined at the hip since University."

"Yes, we are rather a pair," Jane agreed with her husband. "It's just one of those things that God worked out for us, sort of a Jonathan and David thing."

Time passed quickly for them as they talked and shared, and the guests started to leave, one by one. At the end of the evening, James drew Charlie aside for one moment and handed her a large package. "This came from your grandfather's solicitors this morning," he said. The package from Briggs and Smith, Q.C. was quite heavy.

"I wonder what it is?" asked a puzzled Charlie.

"Well, whatever it is, you can open it at the hotel," David said, looking at his watch. He turned to James: "I hope you don't mind, but I have to take this young lady home. The pumpkin has to get her to the church tomorrow morning at eight."

James laughed, "Off you go then," he took Charlie's hand and kissed it. "You are going to do wonderfully tomorrow. I'm very proud of you."

Charlie hugged him and kissed his cheek. "You are very sweet, James. Thank you for everything."

They said good night to everyone and left the Consulate. "They are really wonderful people, Charlie," David said as they were leaving. "Very down to earth."

"Yes they are," Charlie said quietly, fingering the package in her lap. She wondered when she was going to be able to tell David about her concerns about Bryan.

Now was not the time, but she would need to do it soon. Deep in her heart, Charlie knew that it was just a matter of time before another murder would happen. Lives were at stake, and it was up to her to save them if possible. She fell asleep thinking about that.

David drove back to Compton while Charlie dozed in the front seat. He glanced over frequently and looked at her. Charlie was so beautiful, so angelic when she slept. He reached over and gently stroked her face. She roused up and pressed her cheek into his hand.

It was almost eleven-thirty by the time they got to the hotel. Charlie woke up and stretched. "Why did you let me sleep?" she said." I should have stayed awake and kept you company."

"Just having you around is company enough for me. I love looking at your face when you sleep," David said as he stepped around to open her door. Charlie climbed out and into his arms. They held each other for a long moment.

"Charlie, are you really worried about tomorrow?" David held her close, and she looked up at him.

"No, not anymore, David," she kissed him in reply. "You are going to be there for me, and as long as you are there, I can do this."

She reached up and stroked his face. "You have such a strong, kind face, David," she said. "I am so glad that you have come into my life." She settled back into his arms for another moment. Finally, she sighed and kissed him one more time.

"I need to go to sleep, David," she said. David kissed her and nodded.

"You're right," he said. "Tomorrow is going to be a busy day for us." He gave her one final kiss. She walked up to the door and blew him a kiss.

"Good night, David," she said, opening the door and walking through it.

David watched her go through the door, wondering when the dream was going to end. Never, he hoped.

7

David woke to the sound of his phone ringing at six-thirty. It was Charlie, asking him to pick her up at the hotel. He showered, dressed, and was over at the hotel by six-fifty. Charlie was already waiting for him, dressed in a simple knee-length black dress. The only adornment she had on was the Celtic cross around her neck.

David opened the door of the car for her. As Charlie stepped in, she gave him a quick kiss. "Good morning," she said softly.

Charlie had not opened the package that night; there was enough in her life at that moment without adding any more surprises. They drove to the church, not saying a word, just enjoying each other's company in the quiet Sunday morning.

They reached the church in just a few minutes. David turned off the motor. "We're early," he said. "Do you want to go somewhere for a cup of coffee before the service?"

Charlie looked at him, "No David, let's go inside."

They got out of the car, walked up to the front of the church, and unlocked the door. The inside of the church was bathed in early morning glory. The light from the eastern rose window sent a riot of color cascading down to the cross over the altar. The narrow windows in the walls sent lance points of multicolored light into the center of the church.

The sense of peace was overwhelming. "God is here," David said in hushed tones, walking towards the front of the church. He continued up the aisle for several seconds before he realized that he was walking alone. He turned back towards the doors, searching for Charlie.

She was standing at the entrance to the church, trembling. "I can't do this, David," Charlie whispered. "I'm so afraid. I can't go before these people and preach today. I'm not worthy. I need to listen, not lead."

David walked down the aisle to her. Putting his arms around Charlie, he held her close. "Charlie Warren, if anyone could get up before this congregation and minister to them, you are the one. You have a servant's heart: a heart full of love for God and for his people. He's going to help you deliver that message today. You are going up there because these people asked you to. Out of your love for God, and your love for people, you said yes."

His words strengthened Charlie, and gave her peace. David took her down to the front of the church. They sat down on the front pew.

He took her hands in his. "I want to tell you what a difference you've made in my life. Before you came into my life, I hated God for taking Karen from me. I know better now, thanks to you. Karen believed in Christ, and because she did, she is not dead. I love Karen, and I also love you. The two loves are not at war with each other. They strengthen and enhance each other. That is a miracle from God, and you were the agent of that miracle."

David's hand touched the Celtic cross around her neck. "You are my perfect gentle lady knight," he said quietly. Charlie reached out to him, and they held each other for a long time in the holy quiet of the church. They prayed together in silence, then out loud for each other, for the people of the church, and for Angus.

At around eight, the vestry members arrived, along with the other people who would assist in the conduct of the service. Charlie asked some technical questions about their order of worship, who was to do what, the hymns being sung, and so on. As they talked to her, David could see her growing in confidence. It was strange seeing Charlie not at complete ease in a situation, but she was rapidly becoming more at ease with each passing moment.

The church started filling up with people. As promised, Lady Margaret was there, along with her family. The Rossons came in, accompanied by the Davis tribe, who were on their best behavior (on pain of death, courtesy of their mother). David noticed that practically every off-duty cop and his or her family showed up that morning.

Charlie had disappeared into the back of the church to dress for the service, so she missed all of the arrivals. David went hunting for her, found her in the back room, and showed her through the partially opened door all of the people out in the sanctuary. "Everyone out in that sanctuary loves you, and is praying for you." He kissed her.

She returned the kiss, and then backed away from him so that he could see her. "How do I look?" she asked. She was clad in a simple surplice, which hung to her ankles. Around her neck was a green stole with a cross of gold at either end.

"You look wonderful." He kissed her one more time before he left her in the room to pray.

David went around and sat in the pew next to the front. The altar boys came forward to light the candles on the altar, the organist played a Bach prelude, and the service began.

Charlie did wonderfully, leading the people in their prayers and in the singing of the hymns. She led the service as though she had done this all of her life. The church was filled with light and music and the sounds of human voices lifted up in prayers and praise to God.

Finally it was time for her sermon. Charlie came forward to the pulpit. The silence in the church deepened as her strong young voice rang out among the stone columns and oaken beams.

"My brothers and sisters in Christ," Charlie began. "Three times in this past week, the church of God has been assailed by the forces of evil. Less than a week ago, a young girl was brutally murdered not twenty feet from where I am standing. The pastor of this church was struck down with a life threatening illness not once, but twice, in the space of these past few days. This is the work of the devil. Satan has tried to destroy this church, by desecrating this holy ground, and by assaulting its minister."

Charlie paused for a moment to let her words sink in. She gathered her strength, and continued: "In earlier times, a church such as this would have been closed until it was reconsecrated, since a murder had taken place within its walls. But today, this house of

God is open and filled with people, and the reason is that we are at war, and when one is at war, some things must be set aside because of the desperate circumstances facing the church today.

"I was called to be here by the lay leaders of your church because there was no other minister available to preach to you. As I told a dear friend before all of you arrived, I would be far more comfortable listening to the service rather than leading it."

She opened her Bible. "The text for my sermon is a simple one: a single verse from the Book of Psalms: 'The Angel of the Lord encampeth about them that fear him and delivereth them.' The Angel of the Lord is the physical manifestation of God, as he was known to the people of ancient Israel. He was and is their deliverer, their savior. We know him as he was made known to us as the Son of God, Jesus of Nazareth. He is the one who encamps around us, protecting us from evil as a ring of soldiers circle around a precious and holy thing.

"Diseases and disasters will come to us, as they come to all people, but not final and utter destruction, because Jesus has saved us from that. We have put our trust in him, and his shed blood covers us over, protecting us from the destroyer of souls.

"My dear godfather, Angus McKendrick, is your pastor. Evil has struck at him three times in the past week. His church may have been desecrated, and his body may have been injured, but his soul is saved, because Jesus has saved him.

"We are at war with evil, my brothers and sisters. The battle rages around us, and in us, and will do so until Christ comes again for the final and ultimate cleansing of this world. We cannot prevail against the forces of darkness arrayed against us, except through the power of Jesus. That is why, my friends, that your minister was attacked, and your house of worship was desecrated.

"The devil is afraid of you. He is afraid of Jesus and his church. The devil knows that his time is short, and getting shorter with every passing day. This knowledge goads him into desperate acts against God's people, and against God's church. Such acts are proof that the time for evil to triumph and terrify in this world is fast drawing to a close. Jesus said that the gates of Hell would not prevail against his church. Christ himself defends his church, and his people against the attacks of Satan.

"The church is not a social club. It is a base camp for soldiers in a spiritual war. We are at war with evil in this world. It is a fight to the death. There is no quarter, granted or taken in this conflict. Christ is our captain, and we are his soldiers.

"The power of Christ is in you. Stand therefore against the evil that you see. Do not run away, for God is with you. Jesus encamps around you. Amen"

Charlene Warren stood for a minute, letting the final echoes of her words reverberate in the air, and then she sat down. The service concluded a few moments later. Charlie stood at the door and greeted everyone who came out. All of her friends complimented her on her fine message. The vestry members were absolutely ecstatic over how well everything went. Mr. Morton spoke for all of the members when he said to Charlie, "We are so glad that you came. Please come back and worship with us again as soon as you can."

At last the church was empty except for her and David. Charlie sat down and relaxed. David came up to her and sat down next to her. "Carl wants to take everyone to dinner. I recommended Angelo's place, so as soon as you get dressed, we're expected there."

Charlie let out a gust of air and smiled and put her hand in David's. "I'll be right out," she said. A few moments later, the church was locked and they were on their way to Angelo's. Almost the entire church had arrived at the restaurant by the time they got there. Angelo and his family had just arrived from Mass, so the restaurant was not completely ready to receive customers. Carl had called him the night before and told him about Charlie and the special day at Trinity. Angelo was delighted to help. He made a point of introducing his mother and father to Charlie. She in turn thanked them for their grace and hospitality in Italian.

It was a wonderful time. The restaurant was filled with laughter and voices. Charlie and David sat next to Carl and his family on one side of the table, and James Rosson and his family on the other side.

Mr. Morton came up to the table. "Dr. Warren, if you ever decide to relocate to America, and happen to wind up in Compton, I think we could probably have you appointed as a deacon in our church with very little trouble."

Charlie blushed at the compliment. "I appreciate your generous praise Mr. Morton. By the way, my name is 'Charlie', not Dr. Warren. You all have been so patient and kind to me. It was the greatest honor in the world to speak at my godfather's church. I will never forget your hospitality and your patience in putting up with a rank amateur in your pulpit."

Lady Margaret Wilson came up to the table. "I echo Mr. Morton's sentiments. I might add that I intend on sending a message to the Archbishop of Canterbury to inform him that one of his deacons did a marvelous job substituting for Father McKendrick over here in America."

"Thank you, Lady Wilson," Charlie said humbly. "I am not worthy of such an honor, but thank you anyway."

The meal ended, and everyone went home to enjoy the rest of Sunday. Charlie and David went back to the hotel. David was to go on watch at six that evening, so he needed to get back home and rest for a while. Charlie told him that she needed to rest awhile herself. She excused herself after kissing David goodbye, and then went upstairs to her room. David drove back to his house for a much-needed nap.

Charlie went up to her room and closed the door. She felt like a coat of lead had just been removed from her shoulders. Across the room, the package from the solicitors waited. Charlie knew that now was the time to open it. Bringing it to her bed, she unwrapped the brown paper surrounding the box.

Opening it, she discovered that it contained a book with a letter on top of it. The letter was from her grandfather, and was dated November 2001.

This letter is addressed to the sole surviving child of my family. The book contained in this box is the record of our family's struggle with a monstrous and terrible evil. My own son has now been declared dead by Her Majesty's government. We believe he was killed by Soviet agents in Berlin, several years ago, but this cannot be positively confirmed by British Intelligence. Since you are now reading this letter, this burden has fallen to you.

You under an Imperial Commission, issued by Her Late Majesty Victoria, Queen of the United Kingdom of Great Britain and Northern Ireland and the British Empire, to execute the task described in these writings. This Commission is in effect until the task has been completed, or until it has been revoked by the reigning Sovereign of the United Kingdom. May Almighty God protect you and defend you as you take up the cause to eradicate this plague in the name of Christ and the British Crown.

Michael Warren, V.C., K.B.E.

Charlie starred at the letter in her hands, and at the book. It was old, bound with aged leather, with cream-colored cotton paper, which looked almost new. As she leafed through the book, Charlie saw that parts of it were written in two different hands. The first entry was dated September 1927:

I, Charles Warren, write this letter dated September 8, 1927, the 86th year of my life on this earth. Today I have received word that my only son David has perished over in what is now known as the Soviet Union at the hands of their secret police. He has failed in his mission to destroy the evil that I unleashed upon the world, the evil that I knew and the world knows as Jack the Ripper. This name, which has become a byword for unbridled evil and monstrous cruelty, is a name adopted by a supernatural and demonic presence, which I first became aware of in 1888, when the Ripper murders shocked London and the world.

I was placed under a solemn oath by Her Late Majesty Victoria, Queen of Great Britain and Ireland, Empress of India and the British Empire, never to publicly reveal or disclose what I knew of the identity of Jack the Ripper. I was also bound by Her Majesty to pursue and eradicate that evil. If I failed to complete this task, then that duty would fall to my heirs.

In this, my 86th year of life, it is apparent to me that I have failed the Crown, as has my son. The duty must now be passed on to my grandson, Michael. *If he fails in this task, then it will fall to his heirs. They will be bound, as I have, before God our Savior, and by the Sovereign of the British Crown, to fulfill this task until it is completed, or their life on earth ends.*

Charlie read these words with a growing sense of horror in her heart. Her suspicions of the previous day were being confirmed in monstrous and terrible detail. A dead voice from the past was calling out to Charlie in supplication, asking her to complete a terrible task. She shivered as she continued to read Sir Charles Warren's communication:

I must therefore communicate the particulars of the true identity of Jack the Ripper. As an officer in Her Majesty's Army, I was posted to Palestine early in my career, from 1868 to 1870. During that time, I had the opportunity to participate in the excavations of the Temple Mount in the ancient and holy city of Jerusalem. It was there that I met a young surgeon-lieutenant named George Parkinson. Surgeon-Lieutenant Parkinson became violently ill during our work in Jerusalem. We thought at that time that he had come down with one of the many exotic and deadly diseases that plague the Middle East. He became violently insane, a danger to all who came near him. The course of the illness was so rapid and complete that he was sent home to England to his family with little hope for recovery. Unknown to me at that time, Parkinson, upon his arrival in England, escaped from the ship that had carried him home and disappeared into the maze of slums that was the East End.

Parkinson vanished without a trace, and nothing was heard of him until 1888, when the Ripper murders burst upon the world. I was appointed by the Crown to be the Head of the Metropolitan Police, a task that I personally felt profoundly unsuited for, but as a loyal subject of the Crown I endeavoured to execute to the best of my ability.

The manner and course of these awful events is well known to the public, and I find little reason to go over the sordid details here in this manuscript, except to say that on the terrible day when Mary Kelly was found murdered, we apprehended the man known as Jack the Ripper. That day, November 9,1888, was the day when I resigned my post as Head of the Metropolitan Police, feeling as though I had failed my Sovereign, and my country. As word came to me that the Ripper had struck again, Inspector Abberline came to me with word that a man answering the description of the Ripper had been apprehended at the East India Docks. He was found at the docks by the police, consuming what was left of a human foetus that had been taken from the body of Mary Kelly.

This man was bundled into a police van and escorted to the British Garrison at the Tower of London, where he was incarcerated under the tightest security possible. I went to the Tower to interrogate the man, and I immediately recognized him as Parkinson, albeit older and ravaged by disease and abject poverty. He apparently had been supporting himself as a morgue attendant at the City of London Hospital. In the course of his existence, he had contracted one of the numerous and wasting venereal diseases so rampant among the unfortunates of Whitechapel. He was subject to fits of violent insanity, and the Ripper murders were apparently the latest and most florid manifestation of this malady.

As I interviewed him in his cell, his face and manner underwent several rapid and violent changes. His countenance changed from that of a crippled and disease-ridden man to that of a monstrous and Satanic personality. This transformation brought to mind the accounts of demonic possession as it is recounted in Scripture. I also had the importunity to encounter cases of possession while posted over in Palestine. Parkinson's demeanor and symptoms were consistent with my knowledge of these cases. His episodes convinced me that the personage of Jack the Ripper was of Hellish origin, a demonic power not of this world. As long as this man lived, the safety of the Empire, if not the world, was at risk.

Leaving the Tower, I called upon the Prime Minister and informed him of my concerns. These fears were relayed to Her Majesty, who decided that in view of the monstrous threat this man posed to the security of the Empire, that he be held at the Tower under the watch of the Yeomen Warders for the rest of his natural life, or until he might be delivered from the demonic tormentor who was infesting his body.

The Empire at that time, particularly London was teeming with anarchists and revolutionaries. The Ripper murders had incited and galvanized these people into a frenzy. This was the determining factor, in the eyes of Her Majesty and the Prime Minister, for the holding without formal trial or hearing of the man the world knows as Jack the Ripper.

Unfortunately, Parkinson overpowered and killed his custodians and escaped from the Tower. Subsequent investigations indicated that he may have committed more atrocities in London for a few years after his escape, and ultimately that he fled Britain and went to the European continent. I believe now that he has since died, and that the demonic entity that enslaved his body has entered another unfortunate human host. The events of the recent Great War are probably due in no small part to the influence of entities such as the Ripper on willing and unwilling human beings. I pray that their souls are delivered from demonic torment, and that they are able to free themselves from demonic bondage before physical death.

May my heirs succeed where my son and I have failed. May Christ our Lord protect and defend them.

Sir Charles Warren

Charlie paused in reading this manuscript. She could hear her heart pounding with slow, agonizing beats. Charlie shook her head to clear it and stared out the window for a moment. David was sleeping right now, and did not need to be disturbed. Her head spun with confusion as she tried to reason out a course of action.

The next entry was in a hand familiar to her. It was the handwriting of her grandfather, Sir Michael Warren.

I, Major Michael Warren of His Majesty's SAS and Chief Military Planner for the Special Operations Executive, wish to at this time make known to whom it may concern that I know the current identity of the entity described by my late grandfather, Sir Charles Warren. At the time of this writing, 1945, this entity is currently known as Dr. Josef Mengele, the demonic and hideous doctor of the infamous concentration camp of Auschwitz, located in southern Poland.

In the latter part of 1944, word had reached the Prime Minister, Winston Churchill, that the Nazi government was operating large extermination camps in Eastern Europe. Hideous experiments were being conducted there by a man known as "the Angel of Death" in the southern part of Poland. The world at that time had turned a blind eye and a deaf ear to the cries of the tortured masses that were being slaughtered. Churchill directed us at the Special Operations Executive to mount an operation to capture this monster, and bring him before the world to answer for his crimes.

It was my responsibility to plan and direct this operation. Because of the extraordinary danger of the operation, and because of the Imperial Commission given to me, I assumed personal command of the strike team. My grandfather's diary had led me to suspect that there was demonic power behind the activities of Mengele. This knowledge increased my desire to personally execute this mission.

In March of 1945, we were delivered over Auschwitz by Mosquito bombers modified to carry parachutists. These planes, which were the fastest planes in the world, flew from a secret location in the Balkans to Auschwitz at treetop level under cover of a moonless night. We arrived over our target area and parachuted successfully just outside the camp. On our arrival at the house where Mengele was known to be housed, we found it empty. The demonic entity and its host had been alerted to our arrival and had fled a few hours prior to our arrival. On the front door was attached a note, addressed to me, written in Aramaic script. My team sergeant, Angus McKendrick, translated the note. It mockingly told me that I was too late, that my mission had failed. We made our way to our extraction point without incident, and were flown back to friendly lines.

I will continue to search for and bring to justice this creature that poses as a human being as long as I live on this earth.

Michael Warren, Major, SAS

December 1985.

It has come to my attention that the man known to the world as Josef Mengele died in the country of Brazil in South America *in 1979. His remains have been positively identified. Since he has again eluded justice on this earth, I am forced to conclude that the entity has since taken up with another human host somewhere in the Western hemisphere. I hope and pray that somehow God will allow either myself or someone in my family to find and destroy this creature once and for all. You, the reader of this text, are my sole surviving heir. You are charged before Almighty God to execute the commission you have received from your liege, the British Sovereign.*

Michael Warren, V.C., O.B.E.

Charlie closed the book and looked at it for a long time. She thought of the brave words that she had spoken with clarity and purpose in the church a few hours before. David had called her a knight. Now it was time for her to earn that title.

She thought of her life, which was so unconventional in so many ways. Charlie's family was one which could boast of a long tradition of service to the British Crown, stretching all the way back to the first Crusade and beyond. She thought of her upbringing in the public schools, her interests in unarmed combat and fencing, and later shooting. Finally, Charlie pondered her career in medicine and later forensics. They were choices she made with her life, or were they really her choices? Perhaps Another's hand was guiding her, patiently and steadily through her life, coaxing her ever so gently into a path that finally led to America and this moment.

Charlie thought of David, and the love that was growing between them daily. It was real and deep and genuine, unlike anything she had ever known in her life. It was a love that Charlie knew she could count on, a love that would always be there.

She remembered Angus, and the torment he had been through the last few days, and of his church which flew in the face of tradition and had met in a sanctuary so recently defiled by a murder. These people had been attacked, and it was her sacred duty to defend them.

Now she was under an Imperial Commission issued by the Sovereign of Great Britain. All of Charlie's family had been under this burden, and now it was her turn. It was time for Charlie to end this long legacy of evil and suffering, to settle it once and for all. Too many people had died, and too many had suffered.

She would go to Angus and tell him of her plans. At least she could say farewell to him, in case she did not return.

Charlie came to the hospital at six in the evening. Angus was sitting up in bed in the ICU, watching television. Stacey Michaels was about ready to get off of her shift when Charlie arrived at the door of Angus' room. She was dressed in a black police tactical jumpsuit. Angus saw what she was wearing, and guessed its meaning. His heart filled with dread. Charlie motioned for Stacey to stay for a moment. She showed Stacey a picture. "Is this the man you saw that morning in Father McKendrick's room?"

"Why yes, it is," Stacey said, "who is he?"

"His name is Josef Mengele. He was a Nazi doctor at the death camp known as Auschwitz. He died in 1979."Charlie said grimly. "Thank you, Stacey, for taking care of my godfather. Is he still supposed to go home tomorrow?"

"He can actually go home tonight, if he feels up to it." Stacey replied cheerfully.

"Charlie, my love," Angus said, holding his arms to receive her. "I want to leave now."

"Then let's take you home, Uncle Angus." Charlie said. She took Stacey's hand. "Please pray for him, and for me, Stacey."

Stacey nodded her head. "You know what I saw that night, don't you?"

"Yes, Stacey, I do," Charlie replied steadily.

"You're going after it tonight, aren't you?" Charlie nodded and Stacey embraced Charlie for a second. "Please be careful."

They packed up his things. Charlie had brought a spare change of clothes for Angus. She wanted to have him home in his own place if the worst should happen, she decided. Stacey came back with the paperwork and discharged them from the hospital. Charlie took Angus out to her car, and drove him back to the rectory.

Charlie phoned David that Angus was home. David was just now going on watch, so he couldn't spend a lot of time talking. He sent Angus his love, and then hung up.

Angus sat back in his chair and looked at his goddaughter,

sitting across from him in her black jumpsuit. She was checking the action on the slide of her Glock pistol, making sure that it worked smoothly. Charlie fed a clip into the magazine, and then worked the slide so that the pistol was cocked. Putting the safety on, she holstered the pistol. Charlie was checking her weapon one more time before going into combat.

Angus had done such things before himself, years ago in strange and distant parts of the world. He knew the answer to the question he was about to ask. There was a look on Charlie's face that he had seen before. It was the look of a young soldier about to go into battle. Angus had seen it on the faces of his men in Libya, in Germany, and in Poland. He remembered seeing it on his own face as well. The dearest and closest person he had left on this earth was about to go into mortal combat. This might be the last time Angus would ever see her alive.

"You are going into battle, Charlie." He said it as a statement of fact.

"Aye, Uncle, into battle," Charlie replied.

She told him of the package she received at the Consulate, and the contents of the letter and the book. Charlie shared with Angus her analysis of Bryan's behavior, and how it conformed to the behaviors described in the manuscript, and her readings and research into demonic activity. She presented all the strange and inexplicable aspects of the case of Jenny Thatcher's murder, which became explainable if demonic activity and power were factored into the equation. Finally, Stacey Michaels had confirmed independently that it was indeed the phantasm of Mengele, which had been seen in Angus' room that morning he was first hospitalized.

Angus listened to all of what Charlie had to say. "You believe that he will strike again tonight?" he finally asked.

"Yes, Uncle Angus, he will strike tonight. I plan to go to his house and find his operating room. I will take photographs of it and any equipment he might have. If my guesses are correct, he will have his van there as well. I will challenge him and hopefully arrest him, if that is God's will."

"Can you not call the police with all of this, lass?" Angus

asking, hoping against hope that he might be able to dissuade this determined young woman from doing the desperate act she was planning to do.

"There is no legal proof linking Bryan Stone to the murders," Charlie replied. "Not yet. If I notify the police, Bryan will bolt, and that will be the last time we see him. I am certain he has planned for that contingency. He expects a show of force, not a single person, especially not me. I intend to obtain that proof tonight, track Bryan Stone, and prevent him from killing again.

"I cannot share this with David. I do not think he would believe me at this time. He still loves his brother, and the demon would use his love to confuse him and prevent me from performing the exorcism. David's own life would be at risk, and I will not put his life into play.

"Uncle, Bryan's soul is in torment. If I can get Bryan to willingly expel the demon infesting him, then he will be free, and the problem will be solved."

"What you are proposing, Charlie, is extremely dangerous," Angus said firmly. The church views exorcism as an act of last resort. You are sure you wish to proceed with this?"

"Uncle Angus, there is no other choice. I am an ordained member of the church. God will give me the power to do this task. I am trusting in him alone for strength. As a doctor, as a behavioral scientist, and finally as a member of the clergy, I have examined Bryan Stone's case from all of those viewpoints.

"This is Bryan Stone's last and only chance for salvation. I must go and face him, alone. With God's help, he can be saved.

"My family has been under the Imperial commission for over a hundred years. It is my duty before God, and before my liege the Sovereign of England, to execute this commission, and bring this man to justice." Charlie said firmly.

Her words hung in the air. Angus was convinced of the absolute truth behind her convictions. "I won the Victoria Cross in Libya for holding off a column of German soldiers so that our men could be safely evacuated. They knighted me for bravery." Angus wiped his streaming eyes. "What kind of honor can be bestowed upon you who are going to challenge the forces of Hell to single combat?"

Charlie's iron composure cracked for just a minute as he said those words. They both wept and held each other for a moment.

"I need to go with you, Charlie. You must have someone to assist you."

Charlie shook her head adamantly. "You do not have the strength to assist me, although you have the will and desire. I will not risk your life in the performance of my task. You must lead these people, Angus, especially if I do not return. They will need your guidance and wisdom to understand why I am doing this. If both of us die, then there will be nobody left who knows about this. It is my task, and mine alone, to confront the demonic evil that is holding Bryan Stone hostage."

Angus took her in his arms and held her for a long moment. He wept as though his heart was breaking. Charlie held him close and wept silently with him.

"I must go, Uncle Angus," she finally said. The time to go had arrived. Both of them knew it. Angus felt the terrible sinking feeling he had felt in his stomach before an approaching battle. He felt the need to give her one last moment of counseling before she left.

"Charlie, you must understand what you are going up against," Angus said to her in an urgent tone. "If you confront Bryan, remember that the demon inside him will react violently. The struggle between Bryan and the demon possessing him is the crucial battle. You must help Bryan, and address him alone; do not talk directly to the demonic presence. The critical moment will come when Bryan becomes aware of the demonic entity and rejects it. When and if that time comes, you must tell Bryan to turn from evil and embrace Christ. At that point, the Lord will come, and Bryan will be delivered.

"Only Bryan can choose to turn from evil. You as the exorcist can only lead him. You cannot decide for him. Do you understand that?"

"I understand, Uncle Angus. God alone can save Bryan." Charlie replied. "I must help him to reach that point of understanding." Charlie stared down at her watch. "Time is short. Every second I delay plays into the demon's hands, Uncle Angus."

"I know, my child, I know," he said. "Let's go into the church for one last moment."

Charlie and Angus went into the church and prayed for a while. Rising up from his knees, Angus turned and faced Charlie. She knelt down on one knee before him. He made the sign of the Cross over her head. "May Almighty God bless you, in the Name of the Father, and of the Son, and of the Holy Ghost." He kissed her. "God be with you, my dearest child." He reached over and stroked her face.

"I have something else for you, Charlie," he said, reaching into his coat pocket. Pulling out a small Bible, he gave it to her. "This is the Bible I carried with me when I was in the SAS. I wore it in my left breast pocket when I went into battle. Please take it with you now, my love."

Charlie took it from him, and put it into her left breast pocket. "Thank you, Uncle Angus," she said. She turned and started towards the church door.

Angus watched her turn and walk down the aisle, his eyes streaming with tears. Moira had died in the war before they had the chance to have children of their own. Angus loved Charlie as much as if she were his own child. He now knew personally the agony of a parent sending a beloved child off into danger. The sight of Charlie's small figure walking away into the dark night almost destroyed him. He took comfort in knowing that she was ready, and that she was not going out into battle alone.

He turned around and stared at the cross after the church door had closed behind her. "Is this what You felt when You sent Him into the world?" he asked God. The deep silence around him deepened even more, and he knew that he had been answered. He shook his head and knelt down at the altar and wept.

Charlie turned and left the church, going out the front door. She did not dare linger, or she would turn and lose heart. Her heart beat slowly and heavily as she piloted the car down the roads that led to Bryan Stone's house. David had shown her the road to his house that afternoon on the way back from their investigation of the cab. She knew of a place where she could park out of the way, yet be able to get there quickly if need be.

Over her black jumpsuit, she fastened a tactical web vest containing five extra clips of nine-millimeter ammunition. At

Charlie's left hip was a commando knife, along with a heavy flashlight. She also carried a digital camera with enhanced night vision capabilities, as well as a compact police radio.

She parked her car at the secluded location she had seen before. Bryan's home was on a secluded back road, about a mile away from the main highway leading out of town. Charlie moved quietly but swiftly through the darkness, unseen and undetected.

The home itself was a large, two story brick affair, which reminded Charlie of a small English manor. There was a large carriage house standing off to the side. Parked next to the carriage house was a black, late model Mercedes sedan, and a black minivan.

Charlie set her camera to night vision, and took telephoto pictures of the van. Even with the night vision feature, the camera had enough resolution to provide excellent details of the van, even from far off.

The front door to the house opened, and Bryan came out. Charlie knelt down next to a tree. He was dressed in black; obviously he was getting ready to go on the hunt. The minivan engine started, and the motor whirred to life. He sped down the driveway and started off down the road.

Once the sound of the motor receded into the distance, Charlie crept up to the carriage house entrance. Quickly and expertly picking the lock, she went inside. Groping with her left hand, and her gun in her right, she flipped on the switch.

Bryan had converted the carriage house into an operating room, complete with table, ventilator, and monitoring devices for heart rate and blood pressure. Before the table was spread a vast array of surgical instruments. A table next to this contained an assortment of paralytic agents, syringes, and needles. The equipment had a used look: clearly Bryan had gone to various types of sales where used or outdated pieces of equipment were put up for sale. With a limited amount of work, he could get the equipment back in running order. Charlie took pictures of it all, being careful not to touch any of it.

Charlie had analyzed Bryan's behavior as a killer. He was careful and methodical. He would subdue and immobilize his victims, then bring them back here for the final part of the process. Charlie believed that he was not imaginative in his abilities to vary his pattern. At this point, he probably believed that he had not been detected, and his arrogance was his weakness. Her examination of the house took all of five minutes. She turned the lights out, quietly left the building and took up a concealed position close to the house.

8

Two hours later, she heard the sound of a van driving up the driveway. It was Bryan. He stopped the van in front of the carriage house, and opened the back door. Out of the van he pulled a limp body covered with a blanket. It was another victim.

Charlie decided it was time to act. She turned on the flashlight, and identified herself. "Stop! Police! Drop the girl, now!"

Charlie's voice startled Bryan, who dropped the girl to the ground. As he did, he reached for a pistol concealed at his ankle. Charlie was ready for him. She was an expert in knife throwing, and could have killed him on the spot. She threw her knife to disarm him, not to kill. The haft of the knife struck Bryan's wrist, as she intended for it to do, knocking the pistol out of his hand. Charlie drew her automatic and leveled it at his chest.

"Get down on the ground, Bryan, or I will shoot out your knees and drop you that way." Charlie said grimly, advancing slightly to check on his latest would-be victim. She uncovered the face of the girl, who was alive and awake. Her eyes were wide with terror over her tape-covered mouth.

Bryan recovered his composure. "Good evening, Dr. Warren. I see you have found me out. I'm sure you've let yourself into my laboratory, probably without a search warrant, which means in this country all of that evidence is inadmissible."

"I plan on contacting Compton right now and we'll get everything fixed up nice and legal for you, Bryan." Charlie replied. "Get down on your knees now." She aimed the pistol at his knees. "Now."

Bryan held up his hand, and suddenly Charlie was thrown back against a tree. The force of the impact knocked the wind out of her. Bryan charged at her, attempting to attack her from the front. Charlie leapt nimbly to the side, spinning him off of her. She settled into a fighting stance and waited for his next move. Bryan quickly realized that he was no match for Charlie. He ran to the Mercedes, gunned the engine, and raced down the road.

Charlie recovered quickly and called the Compton Police Department. David answered the phone. "David, this is Charlie: Bryan Stone is the killer. I went out to his place and discovered the van he's been using, along with an operating room in his carriage house.

There was a long silence at the other end of the connection. "Charlie, you said Bryan is the killer? How do you know this? What are you doing out at his house?"

Charlie lost her patience: "David, you're going to have to trust me. I found him in the act of bringing another victim to operate on. She's okay. I'm at the house now. Bryan's escaped in a late model Mercedes. Every second you delay in setting up roadblocks increases his chances of getting away."

Charlie's urgent tone convinced David. He replied quickly. "Okay Charlie, I'll have five units out there immediately. Does the girl need EMS?"

Charlie freed the frightened girl and swiftly examined her. "She's not hurt physically, but it's dark out here, and I think you'd better get EMS to transport her to the hospital just to be on the safe side. She's pretty shaken up. "

The girl started to sob hysterically. Charlie tried to comfort her as they waited for EMS to arrive. "What's your name?" Charlie asked.

"Becky," the girl replied. She wasn't more than nineteen years old.

"Where do you live, Becky?"

"I'm from Ohio, originally, but I live in New York City now," Becky replied, growing calmer.

"What happened tonight?"

"Some friends of mine were at a bar, and I got tired of it and I started to walk home. All of a sudden this guy in black comes out of a shadow and grabs me and sticks something in my neck, and the next thing I know is I'm in the back of a truck under a blanket all tied up." She started to cry again. Charlie heard the sounds of approaching sirens in the distance.

"It's all right now, Becky. You're safe." Charlie soothed. "We're going to take you to a hospital and have you checked out to make sure you're all right, okay?"

"Thank you so much for saving my life. You came out of the darkness like an avenging angel." Becky said gratefully.

Several patrol cars along with an ambulance pulled up to the carriage house. Joan Richards climbed out of her crime scene van and started to secure the crime scene area.

"Little girl, we leave you for a minute and you get yourself in trouble." Joan came up and hugged her. "What kind of mess have you caused this time?"

"There's an operating room in Bryan's carriage house, Joan. I had a hunch I'd find it there." Charlie replied. More patrol cars were speeding up the driveway with lights and sirens.

"Right," Joan looked at her skeptically. "I can tell that's all the explanation I'm going to get out of you right now. You can tell me the rest later, sweetie, and I do mean later." Joan turned and walked back to her van and got out her cases. The technicians started to cordon off the scene with the barrier tape.

The medics loaded Becky onto a stretcher, and gently lifted her into the ambulance. "I did a quick exam, and I didn't see any signs of extensive trauma," Charlie told the medics.

"Thanks, Dr. Warren. We need to stop meeting like this. People are beginning to talk," one of the medics told her as he closed the door to the back of the truck.

As the ambulance drove off, David pulled up in a patrol car. He ran up to Charlie and embraced her. Covering her face with kisses, he finally said. "Charlie. What do you think you were doing? He could have killed you on the spot!" His emotions seesawed between admiration and love for this amazing young woman's courage, and violent anger at the incredible risk she'd taken in going up against a killer like Bryan Stone.

Then he stepped back, noting her equipment, "Then again, knowing you, probably not. You look like something out of a spy movie."

"I don't dress in costumes, David. I know how to use every bit of the equipment I have on. Would you like a personal demonstration?" Charlie asked brightly.

"I believe you, love," David replied. "You need to tell me how you knew about Bryan and all of this."

"You need to wait until I can get down to the station, David," Charlie told him. "I need to pick up my car. It's just down the lane where I hid it."

"Okay, I'll drive you down to your car. Go directly to the station and I'll meet you there after I tie up the loose ends down here. Don't worry about Bryan; we have all the roads blocked in and out of Compton." David said confidently as they climbed into his car.

David drove Charlie to her car where she had hid it. David turned off his engine for a moment. "Charlie, lecturing won't do you any good, so I'm not going to waste my time doing that. I know that you have your reasons for doing what you did tonight, so I'm just going to trust you that you'll let me know what they are eventually."

Charlie put her hand in his. "I know how difficult this is for you, David, and I know how hard it was for you to say those things. I know that you trust me and that you are willing to wait for an explanation. It is coming."

He kissed her. "Just get to the station and let us catch Bryan for you, okay?"

"Okay," she smiled and got out of the car.

David turned his car around, and went back down the road. Charlie waved to him as he left turned around and got into her car. She was confident that Bryan would soon be in police custody. The roads would be quickly blocked off, preventing him from getting away.

Bryan had no intention of getting away. As she climbed into her car, Charlie felt an iron arm wrap around her neck and the sharp point of a scalpel next to her carotid artery, just under her right ear. "How careless of you to leave your door unlocked, my dear." Bryan hissed. "You and I are going to David's home now for a little surprise party."

Charlie nodded, "You're taking me to David's house," she repeated, touching the "on" button on her police communicator, keying the microphone. "Why are you doing that?"

"Because, my dear, it's obvious to me that my ham-fisted brother is in love with you, and by torturing you to death, I will be killing two birds with one stone, as it were." he smiled malevolently. He climbed around into the front seat while shoving a machine pistol into her side, and then covered the pistol with a coat. They drove down the private road and turned onto the highway. The lights of the roadblock across the road into Compton grew larger. He pressed the scalpel against her neck lightly.

"We are coming up to a road block, and I am going to pose as my brother," Bryan said pleasantly, as though he was discussing the weather. "Remember my scalpel is at your throat. If you move or say anything, I will cut your throat. You will bleed to death in five minutes. No one could help you. I have a nine-millimeter machine pistol under my coat. It is fully automatic, and I will kill every officer at this road block unless you cooperate. Do you understand?" Charlie nodded slightly.

They drove up to the road block. The officers saw who it was, and then waved them through. They drove through Compton, finally arriving at David's home. Before they went in, Bryan took Charlie's gun, her knife, and her flashlight. After quickly picking the lock on the front door, Bryan marched Charlie into the living room.

Charlie realized that this was her last chance to talk to Bryan Stone. If she could reach him, there was a chance that he might be able to turn and throw off the demonic force gripping him. Charlie started to talk to him quietly and gently. "Bryan, I know what's wrong with you. I know you've been sick for a long time. He's making you do things that you never would do on your own. I don't know how long he's possessed you, or the lies that he's told you. But it's not too late, Bryan. Trust in Jesus. He will forgive you, Bryan, even now. It's not too late."

Bryan pulled her to her knees, forcing her arms behind her back. Using her hand cuffs, he quickly bound her hands.

"Now you are kneeling before me, Dr. Warren," he said in a harsh voice that came from Bryan's body, but not from his mind. "Do you want mercy?" Pulling her hair, he jerked her head back savagely.

"I will never kneel before you and beg for mercy in this world or the next," gasped Charlie.

"Suit yourself," Bryan said, producing a roll of duct tape. He clamped a piece of duct tape over her mouth. Roughly hauling her to her feet, he pushed her down into a chair. Bryan bent over her with his scalpel. "You will scream for mercy by the end of this night, Warren. You will deny God. You will beg for death before I am through. You will live long enough to see me shoot your lover through the heart as he comes home." His voice hoarsened into a feral growl as he said those words.

David had heard every word Bryan had said. Charlie's open mike had alerted him to the situation. As watch commander, he quietly declared a hostage situation on an alternate police frequency other than the one Charlie's radio was set to. All police communications were switched to the alternate frequency, so that Charlie's mike remained open but silent. On the secure police band, he directed the Special Reaction Team to set up a secure command post out of line of sight of his house. SRT members moved into position using night vision goggles to within a few feet of each of David's house doors. A sniper team had set up operations on a rooftop not more than fifty feet away from David's living room window.

Bryan was so engrossed in tormenting Charlie that he failed to close the curtains of the living room window. Thermographic sensors, which provided sharp three-dimensional images of the two people inside the house, were pointed at the house. All of the assets were in place, ready to go. If Bryan attempted to harm Charlie, it would be over in a millisecond.

Charlie knew that Bryan was starting to show signs of wavering. She sat calmly and quietly; praying that somehow what was left of Bryan's soul would rally and gather strength. She looked at him steadily, calmly, without fear. He would not kill her outright. Bryan wanted her alive in order to die slowly.

The demonic rage inside of Bryan became more and more apparent: "I killed all those women in Whitechapel, and then I went to Europe and killed dozens more. They begged for their lives as I tore them to pieces. It was glorious." He turned to Charlie. "But I never got the chance to drown England in blood, thanks to your wretched family. Your collective meddling has thwarted me over the past two centuries, but now, now my pet, you are the last, and you are about to die. But I will go on and on" he laughed maniacally. He came up to her and pressed his knife lovingly against her throat.

"Where, oh where shall we start tonight, Dr. Warren?" he cooed with obscene pleasure. Suddenly a convulsion went across his face, and the malevolence disappeared.

"What, what am I doing? Where am I? What's going on?" Bryan stared about his surroundings wildly. He stared at Charlie sitting in the chair. She moaned through the tape. Her muffled sounds stirred his pity. He pulled the tape off of her mouth. "Who are you? What's going on here?" he asked. Bryan's soul was back in control for a brief moment.

"Bryan, my name is Charlie Warren," Charlie gasped, "I'm a police officer. You must trust me." Charlie said frantically, knowing that Bryan's soul was only in tenuous control and that the demonic presence might wrest control from him in a moment. "You are sick. You need God's help. I want you to renounce Satan and trust Christ to save you. Say the words, Bryan. Believe in him now and be saved."

Bryan hesitated for a moment. He was very confused. "I don't know what you mean. How did I get here? I don't remember anything about coming here." He shook his head in bewilderment.

"You don't need to know all that right now Bryan. Just tell him to leave you in Jesus' name. Jesus will come and help you if you do that," said Charlie. Another terrible spasm went across Bryan's face, and his face hardened into a satanic leer. "So, the weakling came out for a minute, and you talked to him. Well talk to me now, Warren." Bryan wrapped his arm across her shoulders, putting his face close to hers.

Charlie stared into his face, which had transformed into a mask of monstrous evil. Help me, God, to reach him, she prayed silently as Bryan's face contorted.

Bryan flung her out of the chair and onto the floor. His face contorted with uncontrollable fury. Picking her up by her shoulders, he threw her against the wall, pinning her to it. Charlie sank to the floor, gasping in pain.

"You still refuse to bend your knees before me, you little wretch?" he snarled, picking her up and slamming her back into the chair. "Well, it's time for a little surgery." He coiled his arm around her neck, half strangling her as he steadied his grip. Charlie choked and gasped as he slowly cut off the oxygen to her brain… .

At the command post, David viewed the scene through night vision goggles. His heart was torn to pieces in rage and grief as he watched Bryan and Charlie. It was so frustrating. The sniper team was unable to get a clear shot of Bryan without putting Charlie in danger. If an opportunity presented itself, David would call for the breach, and SRT would throw in stun grenades and pour through the door in three seconds. Bryan was just not giving them any opportunity. David calmed himself to be patient. Carl Davis was now at the station coordinating EMS response teams. The ER at Compton was notified of the situation and had alerted its trauma team. The two OR s were manned and ready, along with several other hospitals in the immediate region in case there were more casualties than Compton could handle.

Bryan loosened his grip on Charlie's neck. "Still no pleas for mercy?" he snarled. "Well, maybe you need a little persuasion. Let's see what happens when I start doing some eye surgery." The scalpel started moving towards Charlie's eyes.

"Bryan, trust Je…" his hand clamped over her nose and mouth.

"Shut up!" he screamed, steadying his hand as it paused over her eyes. Then Bryan's hand started to tremble and shake. The scalpel dropped from his hand and fell to the floor as a white-hot bolt of pain shot through his skull. Screaming with pain he collapsed to the floor in a violent spasm, which shook his whole body. The seizure passed, and Bryan slowly got to his knees, gasping for air.

Using Charlie's knees as a prop, he painfully raised himself up. His efforts caused the cross around her neck to suddenly dangle free from her shirt. Bryan stared at the cross, a flicker of hope danced across his face.

Suddenly his face contorted with pain, and then he looked down at Charlie. "This is wrong. I know this is wrong and I don't want any part of it anymore." he croaked in pain and grief.

Bryan knelt by her side, tears streaming down his face. "I'm so sorry, so sorry this has happened to you. Please help me, God help me!" He grasped the Celtic cross around her neck. Breaking the chain as he clutched to his breast, he toppled over to the floor in another convulsion.

"Bryan, renounce him now and you will be free! You are so close! Please!" she pleaded.

Bryan stopped convulsing again and was still. Suddenly, he started to cry.

His breath came in gasps as he cried as loud as he could, "Jesus! Master! Save me!"

Suddenly his body was wracked by a sequence of titanic convulsions. The room was filled with a loud shrieking cry which issued from Bryan's mouth. It was composed of hundreds of voices which reached a deafening crescendo. Then the room was utterly silent.

Bryan Stone lay at the feet of Charlie. He was Bryan again, and he was alive. Raising to his knees, he looked at Charlie in wonderment, and then in understanding. "I am alive!" he cried. " I am free, and God has saved me!" He struggled to his feet, staggering away from Charlie for a moment... .

"Sniper team, do you have a shot?" David asked over the radio.
"We are green."
"Take the shot. All units: breach, breach, breach."

Charlie saw the red light of the laser targeting system on Bryan's back. He was now free of possession; he had defeated and expelled the demon. His life must be spared... .

The sniper squeezed his trigger. The weapon fired just as Charlie moved across the field of fire, knocking Bryan to the floor. The bullet entered her left shoulder and exited out her left chest. The living room exploded as SRT members poured into the room to secure the scene. Bryan was on the floor, convulsing violently. Charlie was beside him, a rapidly spreading stain of blood issuing from her left shoulder.

David stared in disbelief as he saw the chaos erupting before him. "EMS! Move in! We have a hostage... I mean an officer down. I say again, we have an officer down. Shots fired, repeat shots fired. SRT leader, give me a report. Over."

"Watch commander, this is team leader. The scene is secure. I have an officer down, gunshot wound to the left shoulder. Medics are treating. Subject is down and appears to be convulsing. Notify EMS that I have two, I say again two, victims from the crime scene to transport from the scene."

Carl Davis broke in over the traffic. "SRT leader, watch commander, this is command headquarters: Compton ER is on trauma alert. Two OR teams standing by, over."

The SRT medic responded a few moments later. "Watch commander, command HQ: medics on scene request Compton ER stand by for two patients. Patient number one is a female surgical patient with a gunshot wound to the left shoulder. Age: thirty one, weight: fifty kilograms. We have two large-bore IVs established at this time with normal saline running wide open. I have absent breath sounds on the left chest, and I suspect she has a pneumothorax. Patient is awake and alert on the scene. Our second patient is a thirty-three year old male, weight seventy kilograms. This patient is actively convulsing, We are unable to establish an IV at this time, do you copy, over?"

Compton ER broke into the transmission. "SRT medic, this is medic control: be advised that we are standing by for your patients. Place a flutter valve in this patient's chest to relieve the pneumothorax. First patient is to be transported immediately to OR. Second patient is to go to the ER. Do you copy? Over."

"Roger medic control, ambulances are now on scene for transport."

David beat the ambulances to the scene. All he wanted to see was Charlie. At last they wheeled her out. She was pale and in pain, but she was alive. "David," she gasped, her breathing short and painful, "Bryan's all right. He won, David, he won." she lay back on the stretcher and gasped painfully.

Bryan came out next on another stretcher. He was wrapped in a blanket, wearing an oxygen mask. He was still clutching the Celtic cross in his hand in a grasp impossible to break. The medics loaded him onto a second ambulance. David glanced at him and then got into his car, and following both of the ambulances away as they screamed into the darkness.

Charlie kept floating in and out of consciousness. She knew that she had been shot, and that her lung had collapsed. "I'm so cold," she told the medic who was in the back of the ambulance.

"I know, honey, I know," the medic who was treating her said. Her own voice was hoarse with grief as she summoned every ounce of professionalism to treat Charlie. The medic swiftly inserted the large bore one-way valve into Charlie's chest, relieving some of the trapped air that was collapsing her lung. A great jet of air mixed with blood came out. Charlie moaned slightly as the medic did the procedure. Her lack of response to this painful procedure alarmed the paramedic.

"Get this rig moving!" She yelled at her partner. "We don't have much time." After taking a fresh set of vital signs, she keyed her mike to speak to the Compton ER. "Compton ER, Compton ER, this is Medic 31. Flutter valve has been placed the patient's left anterior chest wall with air and blood coming out. Patient's level of consciousness is deteriorating. Her blood pressure is 80 over palpation; her heart rate is 140 and I can no longer palpate a radial pulse."

"They're losing her," Mitch Evans, the cardiothoracic surgeon said, pacing nervously in front of the Compton ER emergency entrance. "I want four units of uncrossmatched O negative blood down here right now. Put the first two units in the trauma infuser. Get me a thoracotomy tray set up in the trauma room. We need to place a chest tube in her now, or this kid's not going to make it to the OR." The ER staff scurried to complete the preparations for the arrival of the patient.

The ambulance screeched to the front of the door. The ER staff tore open the door and helped the medics unload the stretcher out of the ambulance. "Trauma room!" commanded the charge nurse, holding two of the IV bags as they rushed through the entrance into the ER. The surgeon was already gowned and gloved. The medic gave her final report to him as they placed Charlie onto the

153

treatment bed. The rest of the team quickly connected her to the monitoring equipment and removed her clothing.

David arrived through the back door just in time to see her carried into the trauma room. "How's she doing?" he asked one of the medics.

"Not good, Detective," he replied. David looked at the ambulance. The floor was covered with blood. "The slug must have nicked a blood vessel as well as collapsing her lung. We put in a flutter valve to stop her lung from collapsing further, but she's lost a lot of blood."

"Okay, thanks," David got onto his cell phone. "Carl, this is David: I'm at the hospital, and it looks pretty bad. Notify James Rosson at the Consulate and give him an update. He needs to get down here right now. I'll stay here and let you know how things are going."

"Okay buddy, hang in there," Carl said, grief registering in his voice. "We're all praying for her, and she's got you down there by her side."

"I'll let you know as soon as I find out anything more, Carl," David said hoarsely.

The second ambulance with Bryan Stone pulled up. Bryan was seizing constantly, his body straining against the restraints. "Take him to bed four," one of the ER nurses directed. David followed Bryan's stretcher into the main treatment area. Maggie White came up to him.

"Detective Stone, I'm Dr. White," Maggie shook his hand firmly. "I know this is a terrible time for you. My staff is the best, and Mitch Evans is one of the best surgeons I've ever seen. We're going to give Dr. Warren and your brother the best care possible."

"I know you will Dr. White," David said. "What can be done for Bryan?"

"He's seizing constantly, and we'll put in an IV. I want to do a CT scan on his head to find out what's going on with him. Do you know anything about his medical history? Has anyone in your family ever had any seizures before? Is there any history of brain tumors?"

"No, not that I know of," David replied, shaking his head. One of the nurses came up to David and handed him Charlie's gear that she had been wearing. David mutely took it. "Thank you for what you are doing for them," he told Dr. White. He went out to his car and put the gear in his trunk, and then went back to the waiting room to keep vigil.

About half an hour later, Dr. White came through the door. David stood up as she approached.

"Detective, we've managed to control your brother's convulsions," Dr. White began. "The CT scan showed a massive tumor growing in one of the frontal lobes of his brain. We need to send him immediately to a hospital which has a neurosurgeon on staff. Do we have your permission to do that?"

"Of course you do," David quickly said. "How is Charlie doing?"

"Mitch was able to put in a chest tube down here in the ER and give her some blood. That bought her enough time to get her to the OR to allow him to treat the gunshot wound." Maggie explained. "She's in the OR right now, so that's all we know at this time."

"Thank you, Dr. White for all that you and your staff are doing. I really appreciate it."

"She's a very brave woman, Detective," Maggie said. "I understand she knocked your brother out of the way to prevent him from getting shot. If she hadn't, he'd be dead by now."

David nodded mutely. Maggie smiled and returned back to the ER. James and Jane Rosson came into the waiting room just as she left. David filled them in on the situation, and all of them went up to the waiting room outside the OR, which was on the same floor as the ICU.

After about an hour of waiting, Mitch Evans came to the waiting room. "Charlie Warren is an amazing woman," he told David and the Rossons. "The bullet passed through her body, grazing the subclavian vein and nicking the top of her left lung. That's what caused the lung to collapse. I was able to repair the vein and the hole in her lung. She lost a lot of blood, but we've corrected that. She's spending the night in the ICU, and if she's stable, I'll transfer her out onto the main surgical floor sometime tomorrow."

"She's being recovered in the ICU. In a little while, I'll let you all come back for a few moments. She wants to see you, Detective, and her uncle Angus."

"Thank you for everything, Doctor," James Rosson said, shaking Mitch's hand.

"It's my pleasure," replied Mitch Evans, grinning tiredly. "I haven't done a trauma case like that since I was in the Gulf during Desert Storm. She'll be fine. I'll let the nurse know to come get you when she's out of recovery." He turned and went back into the OR.

James and Jane both hugged David. "Thank the Lord she's going to make it," breathed Jane tearfully. David was so glad that they were both there for Charlie.

"I need to go get Angus," he told them, "He needs to know how things went."

"We stopped by at the rectory to see him," James told David. "Angus said that he could not leave his church until he knew something more definitive. He said that Charlie ordered him to stay there."

"That sounds like Charlie," observed Jane, drying her eyes. "When that girl gets well enough, I'm going to turn her over my knee. The idea, running off like she's playing some sort of knight and dragon game!"

"You're going to wait in line for that sort of thing, Jane," David said. "I'll be back soon."

The sun was coming as David, bone tired and weary, drove over to the church. The front door was open. Going through the door, David saw that the church was filled with people. They were in the pews, praying. Angus McKendrick came up to David. "David, Carl called me and told me what was happening. James and Jane also came by about half an hour ago. I notified the people in the church for prayer. I told them that I would be down at the church praying this morning. I opened the church at three. There were already people out front waiting to get in. They've been here ever since." His eyes pleaded with David. "Is she alive?"

"Yes, Angus, she is alive. She lost a lot of blood, and they had to take her to the OR, but she made it, thanks to them," David indicated the church members praying. "I have never seen so much love poured out for anyone before," he said with wonder. "Angus, she's asked for you. I'm here to pick you up."

David hesitated for a moment, "Angus, I need to talk to you, now."

Angus wanted to get to Charlie as quickly as possible, but the tortured look on the young man's face told him that David needed to be ministered to right now. "Come with me to the rectory," he said.

Inside the rectory, David sat down. For a long moment, he said nothing, then he started to talk, in a voice wracked by grief and pain. Angus sat beside him as David poured out his agony. "You told me that it was my job to watch over Charlie, to make sure that no harm came to her. I failed, Angus. I failed you, and I failed Charlie. I lost my wife three months ago, and now I almost lost Charlie tonight because of my carelessness."

David started to weep, his body shaking with tortured spasms of grief. All of the pain of the loss of Karen, and the near loss of Charlie tonight overwhelmed his soul in a tidal wave of pain. David cried in terrible keening wails as the grief poured out of him. He had never wept this way ever before. The part of him that had held his emotions in rigid control after Karen's death was swept away like a castle of sand before an approaching tide.

Angus said nothing. He just held onto the shaking body of his friend as the terrible storm of sorrow flowed out of his body. David had reached a turning point, and the grief in his soul must be purged from it, or he would lose his mind. David was not indulging in an orgy of self pity; he was fighting to save his sanity. Dear God, Angus prayed, help me help David. Restore his spirit and bring him back to life for his sake, for Charlie's sake.

At last the wave of grief ebbed and died away, and a holy peace took its place in David's soul. He entered the presence of Someone who had always been there, waiting to heal him, but would not override his will, as long as David held himself aloof from his pain. He felt the rents in his soul being mended, stitch by patient stitch, by a Physician infinitely loving and tender. The process was done with such rapidity and skill that it was done before he was aware of its presence.

David finally drew a long, shuddering breath. The light in his eyes had returned. He was sane and whole again. "There's a young lady at the hospital waiting for us," David said, rising up from his chair.

"Aye, lad, that she is," Angus said, rising up from his seat. "There's a church full of people who need to know how she is. I must go tell the people."

Walking from the rectory to the church, Angus made his way down the aisle to the front of the church. Turning to the congregation he said, "Brothers and sisters, I have news: our brave sister, Charlie Warren, has successfully made it through surgery. I have been summoned to her side. When I have more news, I will come to you again. This church, your church, is open for you. Please stay as long as you like. Thank you for your love and support."

"David, laddie, I need to get one more thing before we go, please wait." Angus disappeared into the rectory, and was out one minute later. They drove the few short blocks to the hospital. Angus bounded out of the car and raced for the elevator. David had never seen a human being move so fast.

He finally caught up with Angus at Charlie's bedside. He was sitting in a chair at the head of her bed, sobbing uncontrollably in Charlie's arms. Charlie was stroking his white hair as much as she could. Her left arm was in a sling and there was a chest tube bubbling away on the left side of her bed.

"Angus, dear Angus, it's all over," she whispered to him. "I'm fine. We've won. God has won."

Angus raised up his tear streaked head and kissed her hand. "Dearest, I'm so glad you're alive. He glanced up and saw David. "I'll leave you two for a moment," he said, going out the door.

David sat carefully on the bed and looked at Charlie, "Please don't tell me this is going to happen every time I take a night shift. Have James and Jane been in to see you?"

"Yes they have. They had to go back to New York. Lady Margaret was keeping their children while they came down to Compton."

"You know that Jane wants to turn you over her knee when you get better. I can hardly blame her." David said in a teasing tone.

Charlie wrinkled her nose in an impish way. "My big sister: always wanting to look out after me." She played with her sheets for a moment. "David, where's Bryan?" she finally asked.

"He was transferred out to a neurosurgical specialty unit at another hospital as soon as he was medically stabilized. His CT scan showed a rapidly growing, malignant tumor in one of his frontal lobes." David said quietly. Charlie had told him of Bryan's fight against the demonic presence. All of his prior resentment towards Bryan had melted away into pity and quiet sorrow.

Charlie was drifting back off into sleep now. She needed rest, not excitement and company. "David, promise me you'll go to him. There isn't much time left," she murmured as she fell asleep.

David bent over her and kissed her. "I promise," he said. Angus came back into the room.

" James just called me from the Consulate," Angus said quietly. "There's a whole truck load of flowers and tributes headed this way. This girl is rather popular, you know."

"I'm beginning to find that out," David said. "Well, I'm going to go now and visit Bryan. Are you staying with her?"

"No," said Angus, "the lamb needs her rest, I think." He turned to leave, and then suddenly remembered something. Turning around, he pinned something to the sheet next to the left side of her chest. Bending down, he kissed her forehead, and then left the room.

On the sheets, resting over her heart, was Angus' Victoria Cross.

David drove the thirty miles to the medical center where they had taken his brother. CT and MRI scans had shown the tumor to be inoperable. Bryan was in a deep coma. His heart was still beating and he was able to breathe without a ventilator, but he was completely unresponsive. The neurosurgeons had told him that there was little they could do for him. The tumor was wildly malignant, spreading so fast and deep into his brain that it was perhaps a matter of hours before Bryan would die.

He reached the acute neurosurgical unit and went to the nurse's station. He asked where Bryan Stone was located. "I'm so very sorry, Detective Stone, about your brother," one of the nurses said. "Such a sad case, and there's nothing we could do for him."

David went down to the room where Bryan was. A single light shone on his bed. There were no monitors beeping, no machines clicking or humming. Everything was quiet and still. David came up to the bed, and sat down next to Bryan. His eyes welled with tears, and he put his head next to Bryan's on the pillow. For the first time in his life, David Stone wept next to his brother.

"David," Bryan said quietly. David looked up at Bryan's face. It was alive with joy and peace. David reached over and took his brother's hand. "I'm so sorry for everything I've ever said or done to you."

David's eyes ran with tears again. "I'm sorry too, Bryan. I've not been a good brother to you. Please forgive me."

Bryan closed his eyes for a second, and then opened them again. "Charlie... is she all right?"

"Yes, Bryan, she's going to be fine." David replied. "I want you to get well again, because I want you to be at our wedding. I'm going to marry her, Bryan."

"I know that, David," Bryan said. "I appreciate the invitation, but I think I will be busy elsewhere."

David could stand it no longer. "Bryan, you've come back to me. You can't leave now. I love you! Please try to stay, please stay long enough so you can see us walk down the aisle."

"I can't, David. I want to, but God is calling me home. You have Charlie to thank for that. She led me to Jesus, David. She fought for me, and we won." Bryan closed his eyes for a moment. "David," he said in a low voice, "you must do some things for me."

"What is it, Bryan?" replied David tearfully.

"You must tell Charlie that I love her, and I am grateful for what she has done. Tell her that Sir Charles and the rest of her family are pleased with her. Tell her that she has fulfilled her commission and is now released from it. Give this back to her."

Bryan reached out for David's hand and gave him the Celtic cross he had torn from Charlie's neck. "Tell Charlie that her mother is proud of her, too."

Bryan's face suddenly lit up with joy. "David! David! Look there! Can't you see Him? He's so beautiful, David! He's telling me that I'm ready now. He's coming for me David..." Bryan's voice faded into nothingness. The warmth slipped away from his body, and David knew that his brother had just died.

David came out of the room after a long while. "My brother is dead," he told the nurse at the desk.

She looked at him with sympathetic eyes, "Yes, we know, we tried to tell you that, but you rushed off to the room so fast we decided to just let you go."

"What are you trying to tell me?" David was very confused.

"Detective, your brother died two hours ago."

David drove back to Compton carefully. He was exhausted with grief and pain. God had granted him a small miracle in allowing him to talk to his brother. He was grateful for that.

His own home was a wreck, besides being a crime scene. Carl had gotten him some clothes and had put him up in the guest room in his house for the time being. David stumbled through the front door, mumbled something to Carl and Sarah, and then went straight to bed. He collapsed onto the bed fully dressed and fell into a dreamless, exhausted sleep.

9

David woke to the light of late morning streaming down on his face. He had been asleep for days, it seemed. This was a miracle for him in two respects: it was the longest David had ever slept anywhere in his life, and it occurred in Carl Davis' house, perhaps the noisiest place on the planet.

"Well, he's finally up," Sarah said brightly. "We were about ready to send in the kids to get you awake. How are you doing?"

David rubbed his neck. "The last time I felt like this was in Ranger school when I slept all night in a swamp. I'll make it. What's the word on Charlie?"

"She was moved to a regular floor this morning, which is a good thing, because all of the visitors and flowers were starting to drive the ICU nurses batty." Carl said. "She asked for you first thing this morning. Angus is already over there."

"I'll be ready in a few moments." David showered and changed into clean clothes. His face looked like six miles of bad road, but he shaved and started to feel better. Carl offered to drive him to the hospital. David declined.

"I have an errand to run," he said, walking out the door. Carl and Sarah exchanged glances. They had been married long enough to be able to read each other's thoughts. This one wasn't even a minor stretch.

"You've gained weight, Carl. We're going to have to get you measured again." is the only thing Sarah said. Carl nodded, and went to work.

After his brief stop, David arrived at the hospital. Charlie was now on a general surgical floor in a private room. He could barely see the bed for all of the flowers which had been brought into the room. Charlie was in bed, minus the chest tube, her arm still in a sling. She looked angelic.

"Good morning," he said, kissing her carefully so as not to lean on the bed next to her arm.

"Good morning," she replied. David told her about his last moments with Bryan. She agreed that it had been a special time for both of them.

"Oh yes, and there's one other thing, Charlie," David said, getting down on one knee. "Charlene Warren, will you be my wife?"

Charlie looked at him with love and adoration in her eyes. "Yes, dear David, I will." They kissed and held each other for a long moment. David then fumbled out a box from his pocket. "The jeweler said it was a bad idea with your arm like that to get a ring at this time, but he told me he'd resize it if necessary." David put the ring on her left ring finger. It was a marquis-cut diamond flanked by two amethysts. "I hope you like it," he said shyly. "If you don't, we can always go back and get something you do like."

"No, I love it. It's perfect," she said. James and Jane Rosson just entered the room. Jane was carrying an oblong box wrapped in gift paper. They smiled knowingly at each other as they saw David next to Charlie, and the ring on her finger

"I guess we're in time for a bit of a celebration, aren't we?" Jane said, crossing over to David and giving him a hug and then hugging Charlie.

James shook David's hand. "You know this creates all sorts of trouble for us bureaucratic types. Seriously, congratulations dear friend, though I have to admit that nothing in recent days has surprised me less. And as for you, young lady," he turned to Charlie in mock severity. "I see some of that SAS training was used to good effect."

He produced a sheaf of messages. "Let me see. Where to begin? This one's good: it's from your grandfather's SAS regiment. You are now an honorary member." He rifled through a few more notes.

"Expressions of concern from the Archbishop of Canterbury. By the way, he will sign off on your full ordination any time you are ready."

"Please tell His Grace that I am deeply flattered, but that is probably in the far distant future," Charlie responded.

"Oh yes, here's the most important one of all," James extinguished the levity in his voice. "Her Majesty appreciates your service to the Crown and her late predecessor. Your commission has been completed, and you have earned the thanks of the Crown.

"Furthermore, you are hereby created a Dame Commander of the British Empire, and are requested to report to Buckingham Palace for your investiture. Congratulations, Lady Charlene Warren," saying these words, he bowed his head. "I might add that since your creation as a knight revolves around matters sensitive to the Crown, the exact details will not be made public. I'm sure you understand."

James took Charlie's hand in his. "Charlene Warren, you are one of the bravest people I have ever met in my life. I say this not as your friend, but as an officer of Her Majesty's SAS. You have earned your knighthood in a deadly trial by combat, and I salute you as a fellow warrior. You are a valiant and courageous young woman."

"Thank you , James," Charlie said, blushing deeply.

Jane came over to Charlie and kissed her, "I'm so proud of you, and I'm so mad at you!" She handed Charlie a long package wrapped in gift paper. "Everyone else brought you flowers. James and I know you well enough to give you something you'd really appreciate."

"Jane Rosson, what kind of mischief have you been up to?" Charlie scolded as she tore open the paper covering the box. Removing the lid, she gasped. In the box was a two-handed broadsword. "Where did this come from?"

"A proper blade for someone who slays dragons," Jane told her. "Years ago when you and I were students at Stratford, we saw this sword in one of the local shops. I remember you told me how beautiful it was and how much you wanted it. When you were not with me one day, I went back to the shop and bought it. James made me promise to give it to you on the day that you became betrothed. That day has come, and here it is."

"It's so beautiful, Jane," Charlie said, running her hand over the polished blade. Jane bent down and hugged Charlie around her neck. Giving in to her feelings, Jane's shoulders started to shake as she embraced Charlie. She wept silently for a moment on Charlie's shoulder.

"I'm so glad you're alive, love," Jane finally said, drying her tears. "I've spent the last day being mad at you and proud of you at the same time."

"You two know, of course, that you've just given this girl a sharp pointed object." David pointed out. "I'm already black and blue from being poked with her elbows."

"Well, you're just going to have to watch your step, mister," Charlie said impishly. David bent down and kissed her. Angus came into the room.

"Is the church available for a Christmas wedding, Uncle Angus?" Charlie asked.

Angus lit up like a Christmas tree. "Christmas is always a good time for weddings at our church," he said, reaching over and kissing Charlie. He shook David's hand. "Now I have a new son to love," he hugged David.

James asked Charlie, "I take it that you will not be returning to Bramshill any time soon?"

"I seem to be needed elsewhere, James," Charlie replied, holding Angus' hand.

"Yes, I would say that you are definitely needed over here much more than in Britain, Dr. Warren," James said. "But do remember that as a knight of the Realm, Her Majesty has not released you from her service. You may be called upon to assist from time to time in certain sensitive matters."

"I am at my Queen's service," Charlie said, smiling.

"And you are at your King's service as well, Charlie," Angus said. "I just finished talking to the vestry of the church. They sent their love to you, and their prayers. They were most impressed with your conduct of the service on Sunday. They want you to come and serve as my deacon. Will you come to Trinity and help us?"

"I will come, if God wants me to do that." Charlie said in a small voice.

"I think you already know the answer to that. I will let them know of your answer."

James and Jane Rosson made ready to leave. "Well, now that we know that we're going to be busy around Christmastime, we need to run and tell everyone the news. Charlie," James said, looking at her intently. "I know this is not the time or the place, but I could use you as well, here in America. Think about it, would you? As you can see, people are already lining up trying to ask you for your time." He bent over and kissed her on the cheek, "I am so very proud of you. Take care." They left the room.

Angus took his leave. "Charlie, you can come and stay with me as long as you like. The vestry gave their approval. You can send for your things from Britain and you can put them in storage until you and David set up your own house, if that's convenient."

"Thank you, Uncle Angus. That sounds perfect," Charlie said happily.

"Now if you'll excuse me, I need to get back to the rectory and excavate the guest room." He kissed her, and hugged David before he left.

Charlie and David were finally alone together. They sat quietly together, contemplating how fast life had changed for them in the short space of one week.

"Charlie," David finally said, "why has all of this happened so quickly? You came over here to America, and in the space of little more than a week, you decided to give up your teaching post in Britain and move here. People would say that it's too short a time to make such a big decision. What do you think?"

Charlie thought for a moment before she answered. "David, I was not happy in Britain. I took the teaching post at Bramshill because it was open and at the time it seemed like the best thing to do. I came here and I was welcomed with love and affection everywhere I went. I am home here in Compton.

"There are important things for me to do here, David, and I am willing to do them. Most of all, I met you, and you, my love, are the chief reason I'm staying. I never want to leave your side, ever again."

Charlie finished, but one final question remained, and she needed to ask it. "David, you lost your first wife only three months ago. Are you sure that this is not a reaction to that loss? I mean, are you sure that you are ready to be married again?"

David took her hand in hers, "That's a question I have thought long and hard over. No, Charlie, you are not a substitute for Karen. My marriage to Karen ended at her death. I love Karen, and I always will, but I can love you as well. Charlie, I feel like this is something that Karen would want me to do, and in a very real sense I feel that she's given me her blessing to do this.

"I told you that when you came into my life I was a bitter dying man. God sent you into my world to pull me out of the hole I had dug myself into. Karen always wanted the best for us, and I have felt her blessing and pleasure in our relationship.

"You love Angus, the Rossons, and Carl and Sarah, don't you? Yet you've made room in your heart for me, and that's because you want to. I have room in my heart for you, and room in my life for you. That is why I have asked you to join me in living our lives together."

She held out her arms. "I love you, Lady Charlene." David said, kissing her.

David left Charlie and went back to the police station. There were a number of loose ends to tie up with the case. Joan Richards and her team had gone over the crime scene at Brian's home. The wealth of evidence in his van and at the site left no doubt that he was the murderer of Jenny Thatcher. Joan grimly told him that they had found evidence of other murders at the scene, and that more bodies might be found once the grounds around the house were excavated.

"How's that little girl doing, Dave?" she asked at the end of her briefing.

"She's fine, Joan," David replied. "She sends you her best. We're getting married in December."

"That was in the cards from the start, Dave. You didn't have a chance, buddy," Joan commented archly. Her maternal instincts went into overdrive. "Just let Charlie know that we'll get everything squared away on the wedding front as soon as she gets out of the hospital."

"I'll pass it along, Joan," David laughed as he said it.

Joan hugged him and kissed his cheek. "Seriously, David, I couldn't be happier. I've been worried sick about you for so long. Charlie is a sweetheart, and I know you're both going to be very happy."

David's eyes welled up with tears as she said those things. "Thanks, Joan," he croaked, heading towards Carl's office.

Carl Davis was in his office, holding his head in a futile attempt to keep his skull from exploding. The media were driving him nuts. "Charlie came in and said she was going to handle all of the media insanity. She goes out and plays commando and gets herself shot, and I'm completely swamped." He massaged his head in misery.

"Relax Carl, she'll be out of the hospital by tomorrow. She promised me she'd take care of it all. I'll give you a hand right now, okay?"

"Thanks buddy," Carl said, leaning back in his chair. "So what was this all about, Dave? Why did this murder happen, and why was Charlie Warren dragged into it?"

David told Carl about the letter and the diary that Charlie had received, and how it all tied into Bryan and the murders. "Charlie thinks that Jenny Thatcher was just the beginning, that murders were going to take place on each date commemorating the Jack the Ripper murders in Whitechapel, culminating in Charlie being the last, most horribly mutilated victim. She confronted Bryan at the ME's office and that threw off his timetable. Charlie spooked him. The letter and package she received on Sunday confirmed what she'd guessed, so she decided to act. Bryan was so filled with rage that she knew he would try to kill again at the earliest opportunity, timetable or no timetable."

Carl shook his head. "She took an awful risk, going out there alone."

"I don't think she was alone, Carl. Charlie is never alone," David said quietly. "I don't need to elaborate on that, do I?"

"No, I guess not. I know what you mean," Carl chuckled. "Do you think Charlie would like to come to work here at our department? Joan Richards was tickled pink to have her around at the crime scenes."

David laughed, "Poor Charlie: she's laid up in the hospital after getting shot through the shoulder. Not more than one day after that happens, people are lined up, asking her to come to work for them. You're going to have to take a number, buddy. She's gotten offers from the Brits, the church, the state ME's office, and the FBI. There's one offer that takes precedence, and that's the one where she's decided to marry me."

Carl looked underwhelmed, "This is news that's supposed to surprise me? It was all over after the first day she came here, friend. When's the date?"

"Christmas," David said joyfully.

"Well that's great. Now, please take care of this media mess for me, okay?"

David took the piles of requests for information from Carl and went back to his desk. He spent the rest of the day making phone calls, answering letters, and plowing through all of the stuff left over from the case. Before David had left the hospital where Bryan had died, he had directed that his body be transported to a funeral home in Compton. He still had to make arrangements for Bryan's funeral.

Reluctantly, he called Trinity Church and spoke to Angus McKendrick.

"Angus," David began, "my brother died yesterday, and I would like you to conduct the memorial service for him. I know how strange a request that is for you to be asked to conduct a service for the man who nearly killed you twice and nearly murdered your goddaughter. If you don't want to do it, let me know."

There was a long pause on the other line. Angus finally spoke, "Charlie has told me of Bryan's heroic struggle against his demonic enemy. He died a martyr to Christ.

"I will conduct his funeral service at the church. Let those who do not want to come not come, but I will be there even if it's just you and me. I will call the funeral home and set up the time. Do you want a graveside service as well?"

"Yes," David said movingly, silent tears streaming down his face. "Yes, that would be good. Thank you, Angus." He hung up the phone, dried his face, and resumed his work.

After what seemed like a thousand year-long day, he finally got back to Charlie in her hospital room. "Man, they sure are making a fuss over you," he said teasingly. "It's like you've single handedly brought in the bad guy and got wounded in the line of duty and all." She made a face at him. He responded by kissing her gently and stroking her hair. "How are you doing?"

"I'm doing well," Charlie replied. "Do you still want to marry me? I really am quite a pest, you know."

"I know, but someone has to put up with you. I want to marry you now more than ever," David said with feeling. "I'm now over at the rectory with Angus until my house is back in order, which should be tomorrow. I have been told to stay out of the kitchen except for getting water from the sink, on pain of excommunication." They both laughed.

"Oh yes, Joan Richards has officially adopted you, and I've been instructed to tell you not to worry about anything in the wedding department. She'll take care of it all. One of her daughters got married a few months ago, so she knows what to do. Joan's a machine when she starts a project, so be warned."

"My family seems to be growing moment by moment," laughed Charlie. "I'm really not used to having people take care of me."

David reached over and took her hand. He tenderly kissed it. "That's because they love you, Charlie. You must learn to get used to that."

She dropped her eyes. "I'm learning, David."

Charlie shifted in the bed and looked out the window for a moment. "Angus called me a few moments ago, David," she finally said. "Bryan's funeral service is set for tomorrow at Trinity. He will be conducting the service at the church and at graveside. Bryan will be buried next to your parents. I'm going to be there tomorrow for you."

David took her hand in his and kissed it, his eyes filling with tears as he remembered his conversation with Bryan. "I spent barely an hour with him before he died, Charlie, yet I feel that somehow in that period of time, we made up for all of those years of estrangement. Does that sound strange to you?"

"No, David, it doesn't," Charlie replied. "It sounds like God's healing for both of you. It was his gift to you, that reconciliation. Are you at peace with Bryan now?"

"Yes, I am," David said. A bit of late summer sunlight broke through the window and illuminated Charlie's face. "You look like an angel. No, you are an angel," David said, reaching over and kissing her again. "I need to go and try to pick up some clothes from my house so I have some things to wear at the rectory. Your little drama scene in my living room turned it into a crime scene and wrecked the place. Joan said they'll have it back in living condition by tomorrow. Thanks a lot."

"That's just a taste of what's going to happen when I come home to live with you after we're married," Charlie said impishly.

"I'll alert SRT so they can be on standby." David said, kissing her once more before he left. He turned around and looked at Charlie from the doorway, "Get out of this place. They need this room for sick people." David left the room, dodging a pillow launched from the occupant of the bed. Charlie heard him call down the hallway: "Nurse: get the sedation and restraints. There's a violent patient in room 206." She giggled and settled back into bed contentedly.

"Well, our little patient seems to be doing just fine," David said to Angus that evening. They were sitting in the rectory parlor. David had helped Angus do some needed straightening up, which he appreciated. They had just finished dinner and were sitting back, trying to make sense of all of the events of the past few days.

"You knew it was Mengele the day you discovered Jenny's body in the church, didn't you, Angus?" David said over his coffee.

Angus nodded. "I thought at first my eyes were playing tricks on me. Michael Warren, Charlie's grandfather, had told me what he looked like. The demonic presence infesting your poor brother's body wanted me to be sure that I knew that it was he who was making his presence known at the church. Taking the form of Mengele was his way of doing that."

David nodded slowly. "This whole string of events was designed to bring Charlie to America, so she could be killed, and the last of the Warren line be destroyed. Charlie said that she knew the killer. I guess her grandfather had told her part of the story."

"Part, but not all," added Angus. "The missing pieces were provided by his letter and the diary. Above all else, Charlie's grandfather wanted to make sure that she had as normal a life as possible. He kept most of what he knew from her as long as he lived. The timing was such that it all came together so that Charlie could help your brother and defeat the demon, even as he was thinking that he had triumphed. Evil's greatest weakness is it's own arrogance. That's what defeated him."

David thought about what Angus had said. "I need to let you know that I could have wrung Charlie's neck when I found out that she'd gone to Bryan's house by herself. Why did she do that, Angus?"

Angus laughed heartily at David's statement. "I do understand, my son. My goddaughter has a very strong head on her shoulders, as you have seen. Charlie went alone, David, because the demon would have seized you and manipulated your love and pity for Bryan. It would have been used as a weapon against all of you. Such things have happened before in exorcisms, and Charlie knew that.

"It would have been my place and my duty to go with her. I wanted to, and Charlie knew that, but she knew that it would have killed me. Charlie had to do it by herself, and take on that terrible burden alone. Only a minister who places his or her life in the hands of Christ Himself can withstand the Satanic onslaught in an exorcism. Charlie did that to deliver your brother from the clutches of Hell, David. She did it with the power of Christ working through that frail little body of hers."

"There's nothing frail about Charlie, Angus," objected David. "She's a pro, just like you, her father, and her grandfather. Charlie stood up to the worst situations possible and didn't crack, not once.

"I was in the Gulf, and I've been in bad situations in other places as well. I've seen men I thought were tough as they come fall completely apart under circumstances half as bad as what that young lady went through the other night. As a police officer, and as a former soldier, I'd say Charlie Warren's as tough as they come.

They can ship in medals by the truckload to heap on her, and it still won't be enough, as far as I'm concerned."

Angus smiled at David. "As a former soldier in the SAS, I concur with your assessment of her physical and moral courage. Charlie is tough, David, but she has a very tender heart, and she's a loving, giving person as well. She went to your brother's house not to arrest him, but to save his immortal soul. Bryan was in torment, and Charlie wanted to heal him.

"You must understand there is a terrible drain on the minister who performs an exorcism, David. Charlie has won, and God has won, but at a price. Remember that when you deal with her. Charlie needs you, and though she may be reluctant to give voice to that need, you need to be aware of it."

"You see, David, you've been doing some saving as well," Angus concluded quietly. "My little Charlie nearly died when she lost her grandfather and brother. For a while I was afraid I was going to lose her too. Then you came into her life, lad, and you've brought her back to me. I will tell you something that I asked God several months ago. No one knows it, except God and me, and now you. I prayed to God that I would be granted enough life to marry my sweet Charlie and her man in my own church. God listened to that prayer, and thanks to you, and him, I will marry you two on Christmas Day. You are her match, David. God has joined you together for the mutual healing of your souls."

"You aren't planning to die after that, are you, Uncle Angus?" asked David. "Because you have to stay around for your grandchildren, you know."

Angus laughed merrily. "First thing's first, lad." He looked at his watch. "Now we both have to turn in. Charlie wants to be out of the hospital first thing in the morning, so she can be here at the church tomorrow for your brother's service."

10

David went to the hospital and picked Charlie up at eight that morning. She changed into her black dress at the hospital and they went immediately over to the rectory. The service started at nine-thirty with an organ prelude. Angus was to conduct the service, and Charlie had asked to deliver a brief message prior to its conclusion. Charlie's decision to speak at the funeral of the man who nearly killed her was amazing. David agreed, and Angus just shrugged his shoulders and said that his Charlie was always full of surprises.

Bryan's open casket lay before the altar. As David looked at the face of his brother, he saw that Bryan had somehow been transfigured. There was a look of peace on his face that he had never seen before. Bryan had fought his battle with death, and he had won. Charlie came up to the casket, and before the casket was closed and the service started, she bent down and kissed Bryan's face. She placed on his chest the Celtic cross which he had wrenched from her neck in his struggle with the demon. The casket was then closed, and Angus came forward to start the service.

It began with the prayers and readings from Scripture. A few hymns were sung, and then Charlie mounted the pulpit to deliver her eulogy. Her eyes swept over the church.

Charlie looked down at the Gospel of Luke, and the account of the dying thief in the twenty-third chapter. "I wanted to say a few things about Bryan today at this service. As you all know, I was there when Bryan finally fought off the demonic presence infesting his body and accepted Jesus. When I look at the twenty-third chapter of the Gospel of Luke, I see that the thief, who had lived his life in a sordid manner, in his last hour of life turned to Jesus. There are certain parallels when I consider Bryan's life, and its end. Whatever the conduct of Bryan's life, we must understand that Jesus saved him, just as surely as he has saved everyone else who believes in him, and what he did for them on the cross.

"I honor Bryan for his valiant fight against his hellish foe. Bryan is the one who defeated the demon, rather, Bryan and Jesus. Jesus is the one who saved him, not me. Someday in Heaven, I will be able to meet him again, and when that time comes, we will embrace one another as brother and sister."

Charlie sat down, and Angus concluded the funeral service. The handful of family and friends went out to the gravesite, next to Bryan and David's parents. Angus read the service of committal, along with the prayers of thanksgiving to God for the resurrection of the dead in Christ.

As they left the gravesite, David turned to Charlie and told her something that he had nearly forgotten in the chaos of the past few days. "When I was with Bryan in the hospital, he told me to tell you that your family was proud of you."

Charlie smiled, "I know they are, David."

They drove back into town, planning on stopping by the police station for a few moments. David turned to Charlie. "I just have one question, Charlie," he asked. "If you become a knight or a dame or whatever, do I get some sort of title?"

"Yes, you get to be called 'Mr. Stone,'" Charlie replied.

"Well that's not fair, is it?"

"Shut up, David,"

"Do you get a castle and lands and all that?"

"I already have all that, David," Charlie said patiently. "It's a pain in the neck. It was Grandfather's and I turned it into a museum. The taxes alone make it impossible for anyone to live there."

"Are you going to get a sword from the Queen when you get knighted?"

"I don't need a sword. I have a very sharp commando knife. Get the picture?"

"I guess so." David was quiet for a moment." I want a horse."
"No. All you're going to get out of this is me." she said, smiling.
"Sold." he said, kissing her.

Notes for the Curious

The town of Compton is entirely imaginary. I have refrained from looking at any atlas to discover if such a town actually exists in New York State. All persons and activities mentioned in this work are completely fictitious except for the following items:

SIR CHARLES WARREN served as the Head of the London Metropolitan Police from 1886 to 1888. He resigned from his post on November 9, 1888, the same day that Mary Kelly was found murdered. He was posted to Palestine as a British Army officer from 1867 to 1870. He died in 1927. I have linked him with the heroine of my story, depicting her and her family as his descendents dedicated to the service of God and the British Crown. Any resemblance between the characters in my story and those persons descended from Sir Charles Warren is purely coincidental.

JACK THE RIPPER is the common name given to the killer of at least five women in the Whitechapel district of London during the late summer and fall of 1888. He was never captured. Parkinson is a fictional character.

JOSEF MENGELE unfortunately is the infamous "Angel of Death" who ran the hideous genetic experiments at the Auschwitz concentration camp in southern Poland. His remains were conclusively identified in 1985.

THE SPECIAL OPERATIONS EXECUTIVE is an actual organization set up by Winston Churchill during the Second World War. Its mission was to conduct clandestine, high-risk covert operations deep behind enemy lines. The use of the British Mosquito bombers to insert my strike team near Auschwitz is based loosely on the spectacular extraction by SOE agents of the Danish physicist Neils Bohr from occupied Denmark.

THE SPECIAL AIR SERVICE is the elite arm of the British Army used to conduct counter terrorism operations, as well as counterinsurgency activities and covert operations for the British Government. Their training facility is located in the Cotswolds in Wales.

Printed in the United States
29483LVS00007B/91